Essays and Dissertations

Chris Mounsey is Senior Lecturer at King Alfred's, Winchester. Author of *Christopher Smart: Clown of God*, a biography of the eighteenth-century poet, Chris is currently working on a biography of Daniel Defoe.

One Step Ahead ...

The *One Step Ahead* series is for all those who want and need to communicate more effectively in a range of real-life situations. Each title provides up-to-date practical guidance, tips, and the language tools to enhance your writing and speaking.

Series Editor: John Seely

Titles in the series

CVs and Job Applications	Judith Leigh
Editing and Revising Text	Jo Billingham
Essays and Dissertations	Chris Mounsey
Giving Presentations	Jo Billingham
Law in Everyday Life	John Seely
Organizing and Participating in Meetings	Judith Leigh
Presenting Numbers, Tables, and Charts	Sally Bigwood and Melissa Spore
Publicity, Newsletters, and Press Releases	Alison Baverstock
Punctuation	Robert Allen
Spelling	Robert Allen
Words	John Seely
Writing Bids and Funding Applications	Jane Dorner
Writing for the Internet	Jane Dorner
Writing Reports	John Seely

onestepahead

Essays and Dissertations

Chris Mounsey

Cartoons by Beatrice Baumgartner-Cohen

OXFORD
UNIVERSITY PRESS

Many thanks to W. R. Owens of the Open University, Dilwyn Knox of
University College, London, and Mick Jardine of King Alfred's, Winchester
for guidance and assistance.

OXFORD UNIVERSITY PRESS

Great Clarendon Street, Oxford OX2 6DP

Oxford University Press is a department of the University of Oxford.
It furthers the University's objective of excellence in research, scholarship,
and education by publishing worldwide in
Oxford New York
Auckland Cape Town Dar es Salaam Hong Kong Karachi
Kuala Lumpur Madrid Melbourne Mexico City Nairobi New Delhi
Shanghai Taipei Toronto

With offices in
Argentina Austria Brazil Chile Czech Republic France Greece
Guatemala Hungary Italy Japan South Korea Poland Portugal
Singapore Switzerland Thailand Turkey Ukraine Vietnam

Oxford is a registered trade mark of Oxford University Press
in the UK and in certain other countries

© Chris Mounsey 2002

The moral rights of the author have been asserted
Database right Oxford University Press (maker)

First published 2002

British Library Cataloguing in Publication Data
Data available

Library of Congress Cataloging in Publication Data
Data available

ISBN 13: 978-0-19-860505-8

10 9

Design and typesetting by David Seabourne
Printed in the UK by Ashford Colour Press Ltd, Gosport, Hampshire

Contents

1 | Introduction

Why an essay?

The essay is a piece of writing designed for academic purposes. It is short enough to be read at one sitting. It communicates detailed information about a subject between people who share a common background of knowledge (experts in the field). In the modern academic world it is often called a 'paper' and published in a specialist journal.

A lot of the work you do at undergraduate level is assessed in the form of the essay. It is long enough for you to show that you know something about a particular subject. It is short enough that your tutor can mark it conveniently.

But an essay written for the assessment of your academic progress is a strange beast. Where an academic 'paper' is a means of communicating new information to other people who share a common background of knowledge, an assessed essay is a means of communicating information to your tutor about yourself, and how much you know. The essay you write should tell your tutor that you have understood the information that you have been taught, and that you can argue about it. **You do not have to say anything new.** You have to show that you are becoming one of those people who share the common background of knowledge.

In other words, you have to write your essays in a specific way so that they will show you off to the best advantage. This book is intended to tell you how to go about writing academic assessed essays.

How to use this book

The book is separated into two sections, A and B.

Part A presents the information you will need to write an essay.

In Part A, Chapters 1 to 6 take you through one method of writing an essay from start to finish: from choosing your question; to gathering information; to writing an argument; to reworking your ideas; to presentation. Chapter 7 gives some hints about how to manage your time so you can make sure your essay is ready when it should be. Chapters 8 and 9 go back through some of the ideas from Chapters 1 to 6 and give more details about various aspects of research and writing. Chapter 10 suggests methods for writing dissertations and long essays. Chapter 11 deals with exams.

Part B gives a recap of the information in Section A in the form of checklists and flow charts. There are also chapters giving detailed help with grammar, punctuation, and references.

Part B runs over the same information as Part A in the form of checklists and flow charts, followed by a reference guide.

When you begin to write your first undergraduate essays, use Part A, Chapters 1 to 6. They will take you through the basics of how to write an essay. You will probably find it easier if you get these ideas under your belt before you begin to work on points for style.

Before we go on to the points for style, Chapter 7 gives some hints about when to start reading, researching, and writing your essay. No matter how good an essay is, if you do not hand it in on time you might lose marks.

The 'points for style' are found in Chapters 8 and 9. These chapters detail what you might do if you discover that certain elements of your essay-writing technique need polish. Use this section when you have written a few essays, or if you have time to go back over your work to make it look really good.

You will have written a good few essays before you have to tackle dissertations (Chapter 10) and examinations (Chapter 11). Both are types of essay, but each requires special skills.

Part B should be used as a checklist for ticking off the various stages of writing. Run through Part B after you have finished each essay you write just to make sure you have not forgotten anything.

Some reading routes	Beginner information	Further details
Your first essay	chapters 2–6	pages 97–103
When an essay counts	chapters 7–9	pages 105–21
Dissertations	chapter 10	pages 105–21
Exams	chapter 11	
Quick reference footnotes	pages 112–121	

This is an essay

The word 'essay', as we use it today, comes from the French writer Michel de Montaigne, whose *Essais* were published in 1580. The Elizabethan scholar Francis Bacon (the man who may or may not have written Shakespeare's plays) brought the form into the English language when he published a collection called *Essaies* in 1597. Since Bacon was arguably the founder of modern academic method, the essay has become the mainstay of academic communication ever since.

Soon after, Joseph Glanvill gave us the idea that an essay is an incomplete piece of work. In 1665 he wrote *Scepsis scientifica; or confest ignorance, the way to science*, in which he argued that an essay was an 'imperfect offer at a subject'. What Glanvill meant was that when he wrote his essay he wanted readers to remember he did not know absolutely everything about his subject. This is important for us to remember too. When we write an essay we do not have the space or time to put down everything there is to know about our subject, so we must not try to be the fount of all knowledge. We are just giving our opinion about a little bit of our subject.

What you are reading is an essay.

The word 'essay' also means 'to try' or 'to test'. In this case, the meaning is derived from metal smelting and goes back to biblical times. The molten metal had to be tried or tested in the fire to make sure it was pure enough, or 'true'. This meaning gives us another clue about how to go about writing an essay, since what we must do is test an idea and demonstrate something to be the case. In other words, an essay is like a scientific experiment, or a court case. It should use evidence in support of an idea.

If we join these two thoughts together—that an essay is an opinion about a little bit of a subject, and that by means of evidence it supports an idea—we come to something like a useful definition of the word 'essay'.

An essay is your opinion about a little bit of a subject, in which you use evidence to support your opinion.

What makes this an essay?

■ It is an opinion.

■ It is based on evidence.

■ It does not claim to say everything there is to say about essays.

> An essay is your opinion about a little bit of a subject, in which you use evidence to support your opinion.

2   Looking at questions

When you start a new topic or module of your degree, one of the first things you will be given is a list of essay titles and the date for handing in. The first hurdle to jump is choosing which essay to tackle.

First we'll consider the sort of titles you might come up against, then we'll go on to how to make your choice.

Specific and general essay titles

Essay titles most often come in two types, the specific and the general. Which sort you get will depend upon your institution and the person who sets the titles. Both specific and general questions should be answered a similar way, since:

An essay is your opinion about a little bit of a subject, in which you use evidence to support your opinion.

Choosing your essay title can seem a bit of a lottery.

Specific essay titles

Specific questions have a narrow focus and will probably name people or situations or problems. Examples of specific questions might be:

- To what extent can it be argued that Byron and Keats are second-generation Romantic poets?

- Discuss the importance of the Tizer brand and its role in the development of the marketing mix.

- Explain Harriet Martineau's role in the creation of sociology as a science.

There is little scope in this type of question. You must write about the people and situations mentioned. But none of the examples has a particular answer in mind: there is no right or wrong answer.

His words ... like so many nimble and airy servitors trip about him at command.
(Milton)

- It might be argued **either way** that Byron and/or Keats were or were not second-generation Romantic poets.

- The importance of a brand name and how it functions in the product's marketing mix is open to debate.

- Whether Harriet Martineau can be thought of as a scientific sociologist, or a sociologist at all, is up to you to choose.

There is still room for your **opinion** in specific questions, though it must be based on the **evidence** you can find.

General essay titles

General questions work in a different way. They suggest the area you must write about and demand you explore the topic from a certain angle, but they rarely mention specific names, situations or places. Examples of general questions might be:

- How great was the influence of women on the development of the novel in the eighteenth century?

- To what extent and in what ways do you think that courts influenced Renaissance culture?

- Evaluate the effect of landscape on the expansion of the town.

There is a lot of scope in this type of question, and they seem trickier to answer.

You might think you have to write about:

- every aspect of all eighteenth-century women's influences on the development of the novel;

■ the influence of every type of court on Renaissance culture in England, France, and Italy;

■ the effects of every different type of landscape on all the towns in the world.

But you do not. **However general the question, your answer must be specific.** The difference with general questions is that you get to choose what you are specific about.

Examples

If you wanted to answer about the influence of women on the development of the novel in the eighteenth century, you might start by deciding whether you wanted to write about:

■ women **writers** or women **readers**.

If you choose women writers, you could then narrow things down further and choose to write on, say:

■ **one** or **two** women writers.

To answer the question on Renaissance culture, you would need to decide whether you were going to write on, say:

■ royal courts or law courts;

■ in **one** country.

To answer the question on the effects of landscape on urban expansion, you might choose, say:

■ **one** or **two** towns;

■ towns with different environs.

Understanding the question

If the questions look difficult, and you are not sure what they are asking, try making a 'translation' of the question into terms that you do understand. To do this:

■ Change only the **variables** of the question and keep intact the **terms** that describe the sort of argument you are asked to make.

Examples of translations

You might translate questions like this, leaving the **terms** intact and changing the **variables**:

■ To what extent can it be argued that Byron and Keats are second-generation Romantic poets?

   Translation: **To what extent can it be argued** that ducks are birds?

■ Discuss the importance of the Tizer brand and its role in the development of the marketing mix.

   Translation: **Discuss the importance of** writing good tunes and their **role in the development of** a successful pop group.

■ Explain Harriet Martineau's role in the creation of sociology as a science.

   Translation: **Explain** Elvis Presley's **role in the creation of** rock 'n' roll music as an art form

■ To what extent and in what ways do you think that courts influenced Renaissance culture?

   Translation: **To what extent and in what ways do you think that** your mother influenced your character?

■ Evaluate the effect of landscape upon the expansion of towns.

*...but if I could understand,
What you are,
root and all, and
all and in all, I
should know
what God and
man is.*

(Tennyson)

13

Translation: **Evaluate the effect of** essay writing on the expansion of your knowledge.

■ How far did Handel's music evolve during his time in London?

Translation: **How far** did Eric Cantona's football **evolve during his time** at Manchester United?

From these examples, you can see that the important words are often the least conspicuous ones.

Here, they are:

■ 'To what extent can it be argued ...'

■ 'Discuss the role of ...'

■ 'Explain ...'

■ 'To what extent and in what ways ...'

■ 'Evaluate ...'

■ 'How far ...'

Each **term** requires that you give evidence, and that you give the evidence as part of an argument. The type of argument you have to make is hinted at by the **terms**:

■ **'To what extent can it be argued ...'** suggests you should evaluate the strength of the claim that is made in the rest of the question. Here, it may be quite convincingly argued '... that ducks are birds'. On the other hand, it could be argued that since not all birds have webbed feet, there are grounds for believing that ducks are a special type of bird. In the case of Byron or Keats it could be argued that 'to no extent' could they be called second-generation Romantics.

■ **'Discuss the role of ...'** suggests that you have to accept the premises of the question, and that you should describe and comment on them. Here, it is taken for granted that pop groups write tunes, and that pop groups try to be popular. There might, however be various different ways of interpreting the importance of a good tune on popularity, and that is what the question is after. You might want to argue that tunes are unimportant in comparison with the style statement made by the group. In the case of the Tizer brand name, you might want to argue that the old-fashioned name is a positive disadvantage in selling the product to young people, but an advantage in selling it to a mature market.

■ 'Explain ...' also suggests that you have to accept the argument that follows. Your explanation will be finding links between the variables of the question. Here, it is taken for granted that Elvis Presley had an influence on rock 'n' roll music, but that you should find reasons why Presley was quite so influential. In the case of Harriet Martineau, you might argue that she was not influential in her time, and it is only from a modern feminist viewpoint that she has been thought to be influential.

I wish he would explain his explanation.

(Byron, on Coleridge)

■ 'To what extent and in what ways ...' introduces a tricky question, since its terms can be read either way. You might argue that your mother did not influence your character at all. She influenced your character in no ways and to no extent. Your answer could go through the common misconceptions about mothers' influence on their children. On the other hand you might argue that your mother was the sole influence on your character. She influenced your character to a great extent and in many ways. In the case of the Renaissance law courts, if you argue that they were the mainstay of Italian society, your answer should give your reasons.

■ 'Evaluate ...' requires that you write about the value of the variables in the question. In our example, you might argue that essay writing contracts your knowledge. Essay writing is of no value to your knowledge. Conversely, you might argue that essay writing is the most valuable way of getting to understand the nuances of a subject. You will have to give reasons for your opinion. In terms of physical geography, after you have given your reasons you might also list other ways of understanding the development of towns (perhaps going into one in some detail) and say why it is not so good.

■ **'How far ...'** is another way of giving you the opportunity of agreeing or disagreeing with the variables of the question. You might argue that Eric Cantona's football did not evolve when he played for Manchester United—his football remained the same. It did not change very far at all. You might argue that it changed a lot while he was Britain. In the case of Handel's musical development, you might argue that, since he arrived in London and wrote one sort of music and left writing another sort of music, his music developed considerably.

Quote and discuss questions

Devise wit! Write pen! For I am for whole volumes in folio!

(Shakespeare)

Another type of essay question comes in the form of a quotation followed by the word 'Discuss'. For example:

■ 'Francis Bacon wrote Shakespeare's plays.' Discuss.

These questions look hard, but follow the same pattern as the others. The term 'Discuss' gives you the opportunity to agree or disagree with the variables of the question. In our example, you can agree or disagree with the idea that Francis Bacon wrote Shakespeare's plays.

What is common to all these questions?

All these different types of question are written so that you can argue for or against the ideas in the question. But remember your argument is your **opinion**, and it must be based on **evidence**.

Choosing your title

Choosing which essay title to answer is now quite simple. Base your choice on these processes of narrowing down the topic, and translation.

If the questions are **specific**, ask yourself:

■ Which people or situations did I enjoy learning about the most?

Choose the question in which they are mentioned.

If the question is **general**, you may have more questions to choose between. However, you must write about what you are interested in, so go for the general question which best suits the people or situations that caught your interest.

Remember
Write about what
most interests you.

Above all choose the topic you enjoyed the most so you will be motivated to be able to read enough about it to find your evidence. Only when you have enough evidence will you be able to argue an opinion.

Which essay shall I choose?

When you get your list of essay questions at the start of the module:

Tip
Oliver Wendell
Holmes used to let
his writings 'mature
in the wood'—he
put them away in a
drawer for a few
weeks, then looked
at them again.

■ Put it away until you've had enough lectures to decide which area of the module you are interested in.

■ Read the required texts for each week.

■ Don't start doing essay work for a couple of weeks.

When you have decided which topic interests you the most, you can start to gather the information necessary to find the evidence on which to base your opinion.

3 Research

A bibliography is a list of books that were read to find out information on a particular topic.

The first place you might think to look for evidence on which to base your opinion is in your lecture notes. **This is not a good idea**. Lectures are meant to introduce you to a subject and some of the debates about the subject. Your lecturers will know the lectures they give very well. If you simply repeat what they said, they will know you have not done much work and **you will not get a high grade**.

Using the library

Bibliography

A better place to look for your evidence is in the books on the reading list or bibliography, which you will probably be given at the start of the module. The list will be made up of the books your lecturer read to write the lectures. When you read these books you will be familiar with the concepts since you will have heard them before in lectures.

More importantly, there will be **other pieces of information** that you can use so your lecturer will know you have done some reading of your own. **This is how to get a higher grade**.

The problem with bibliographies

There is one major problem with bibliographies. Library budgets are small and class sizes are getting bigger, so the books on the bibliography are the first to be taken out. Books need to be circulated among the entire group of students but there are always book hogs who will go to any length to stop books getting around everyone. Remember:

- The best way for books to circulate is to keep them in the library, so try to work in the library.

- If you do take books out, return them promptly when you have finished reading them. You do not have to wait for the return date.

If you follow these ideas, you stand a better chance of seeing the books yourself. Keep mentioning it at your institution's committees, and ask your lecturers to remind other students to bring books back if there is a queue to read them.

Getting around book hogs

You may be able to get round the problem of book hogs since popular books on a topic (the ones on the bibliography) will often be held in your library on some sort of short-term loan. These will vary:

Try not to be a book hog.

- very short loans, where books may not be taken out of the library (four hours is typical);

- for twenty-four hours;

- for a week.

A note for part-time students

The system of very short loans and twenty-four-hour loans can make it difficult for students who do not have access to the library each day, or for extended periods.

The best thing you can do is to try to work library time into your weekly schedule. Two periods of two hours a week is a good idea.

If you cannot, try to use regular loan books if they are available.

If you cannot manage either of these, you might have to photo-copy relevant chapters from the short-loan items. Remember, though, that you can only copy up to 10% of a book.

Student reserve collections

There may be a student reserve collection for the very short-loan books, so find out if there is and where it is.

■ Books might be held behind the main issue desk, and you have to ask for them by title.

■ There might be a dedicated room in the library where all the short-loan books are kept, with its own issue and return desk.

When you get your first bibliography, ask your lecturer if there is a system of this kind, and if there is, go to the library and ask how it works.

You never look stupid asking questions about how to find library books.

Astronomically high fines for late return of short-loan books are usual, so be sure to get them back on time.

Reserving books

If a book is out on short or long-term loan you can usually reserve it so you get to read it next.

■ Go to the issue desk and ask about the procedure.

You may even be able to recall it from the person who has it: another good way to get around book hogs.

The problem with short-loan books

Short loans are all well and good, but the system might fail you: either because the books on the bibliography do not quite match the essay you have chosen, or because there is a long queue for the book you think will help most.

Remember:
There are NO books on ANY subject you ABSOLUTELY HAVE to read.

Do not despair.

You will have to find your own books.

Finding books on the right topic

Finding other books on a particular topic is not as hard as you might think. There are two methods I shall describe here:

■ shelf mark search;

■ keyword search.

Shelf mark search

This type of search uses the number you find on the back of the book, which the library uses to catalogue it, and to get it on the right shelf so it can be found easily. Most libraries use the Dewey cataloguing system, and store books with others on the same or similar topics.

Note
Even if the book you can't get hold of is kept in a special room, since it is a short-loan book, the shelf with the same shelf mark in the main library will house books on a similar topic.

1. Look up the shelf mark of the book on your bibliography that most nearly matches what you want to write about.

2. Write it down.

3. Find the place on the shelf where the book ought to be.

4. Look around on the shelves and you'll find ten, twenty, a hundred, possibly a thousand books on similar topics.

5. Look at the titles on the spines of the books and make your selection.

| **Keyword search**

Another way to find books on your topic, if your library has a computer catalogue, is to do a KEYWORD SEARCH.

Search for:
Antidisestab
lishmentar
nism _

Look for books on distinctive topics by keyword searches

This sort of search is particularly useful if you are working with a topic that has distinctive words in it.

1. Think up two or three words that might appear in the title of a book that will help you.

2. Write them down.

3. Enter the words in your library computer Keyword Search function.

4. Your bibliography will appear.

Note
Experiment with your library catalogue. You need not be looking for specific books, just for books on a particular subject.

Example

You are writing an essay on the Renaissance courts.

1. Choose the words 'Renaissance' and 'courts'.

2. Enter them on your library computer Keyword Search.

On my library computer, titles of twenty books appeared.

The problem with keyword searches

Where your subject is less specific, you might find you get a very long list of titles.

A keyword search on 'physical' and 'geography' produced 436 books on my library computer. If this happens, try adding a third keyword. In the example, of 'physical' and 'geography':

■ Adding the word 'British' gives seven books.

■ Adding the word 'sea' gives twenty books.

The third word you choose will narrow down the field. Your choice of which word depends on your topic.

Other searches

You will find further methods of searching in Chapter 8.

See pp. 62–4

Which books should I use?

There are two basic guidelines you should bear in mind when collecting books for writing a degree essay:

First: if the book is not held at your library, do not look for it elsewhere.

■ Your institution ought to hold all the books necessary for passing your course.

■ Unless you are going to refer to it more than once, buying a book may not be worth it (except when you really like the subject).

Second: if the book is over ten years old, think twice about using it. The ideas could be out of date.

Some books have become classics in their field, but you will know a book like this is all right to use since it will have been republished.

Your tutors have to write a book every four years, so the academic world is moving forward quite fast.

| # Finding relevant information

If you follow some or all of these methods of gathering books on your topic, you will end up with a pile on your library table. About ten books will be enough.

You are now ready to start your research.

■ Turn to a clean page on your pad of paper.

■ Take a pencil.

■ Open the first book on your pile.

Start with the **contents page** where the titles of the chapters are given.

Read them over and decide if one or two seem as though they are relevant to your essay.

If they are:

Note!
Don't start reading yet.

■ Note down the title of the book and the chapter number and title.

If not, turn to the back of the book and look up some relevant words in the **index**.

■ Look for ranges of pages cited (that is over two pages) and ignore single-page citations.

■ Note them down on your pad under the title of the book.

If there are none, or only a few references, put the book aside.

Move on to the next book and repeat the process until you have gone through the whole pile of books.

Your own reading list

You should now have two piles of books, the ones with relevant chapters or passages and the ones that have nothing interesting for your essay. You should also have a list of relevant chapters or passages in the relevant books.

Take the reject pile of books to the re-shelving trolley so that other people can get a look at them in case the books are relevant to their essay. **Remember, there will be a whole group of you working on the same essay at the same time**. **Don't be a book hog**.

You should now have, say, **six** books in front of you.

Each will have one or more chapters or passages that seem relevant to your essay, and you will have a list of these extracts since you will not be able read them all at one sitting.

A note to students with family commitments

If you can, it is best to read in the library. If you must work at home and have family commitments, it might be a good idea to tell your family (spouse and children) that for two hours (once or twice a week) they cannot have access to you. Try locking yourself away in a room and do not answer knocks. You might arrange quality time for children at other times. Try to vary the times you work so you're not always working late in the evenings when you might be tired.

Finding quotes

When you start reading, remember that not everything in the chapter or passage will be relevant to your essay. What you are trying to find is evidence from which you can form and support an opinion. When you find a relevant piece of information, write down the sentence in which you find it verbatim: that is, word for word, together with the number of the page.

The process is not difficult. But a perplexing question will keep coming up in your head—What is important?

Keep a lookout for the really relevant information.

| **What is important?**

The answer to the question is not as hard as it seems.

The important bits of information are those that catch your eye.

You are not reading to find a standard set of facts or figures that are necessary for every essay on your topic. Important bits of information are important because they are interesting to you. If they interest you, you will already have formed an opinion about them (that they are interesting) and they will therefore be relevant to your argument.

This means that if you don't know exactly what you are going to write about, take down anything that looks interesting to you. Note down **on your pad** (do not mark the book you are reading) the sentences or paragraphs that contain the interesting bits, and you will automatically find out what you are going to have an opinion about. **It will be on the page of notes you have just made**.

Example of finding quotes for essays

You are researching, say, an essay entitled: 'How far did Handel's music evolve during his time in London?'

(A question in the **general style** might be: 'How far can Britain be thought of as sustaining musical evolution in the eighteenth century?' You choose to write about London and Handel's music in particular.)

The book you have found that seems relevant is called *The Oxford History of English Music*, by John Caldwell. The extract you have chosen to read is:

Volume 2, chapter 1: 'Handel and his English Contemporaries, c.1715-1760'.

On pages 1 and 2, you read:

The career of Handel in England in many ways anticipates that of a composer such as Mozart in youth or Haydn in his later years in its jettisoning of the constraints of service for the sake of independence and the risks and rewards of catering for the public taste. In this respect Handel's own predilections coincided with the imperatives of English musical life, where the social and political structure did not allow of congenial long-term employment outside the increasingly humdrum routine of the royal court and chapel and that of the major churches. Handel had experienced a mixture of enterprise and short-term employment (with the marquis Francesco Ruspoli) in Italy, and had subsequently become Kapellmeister to the elector of Hanover, later George I of England. On his first visit to England Handel achieved enormous musical and social success, and this must have encouraged him to return, ostensibly for a second short visit, in 1712. Encouraged by his ready acceptance (he was given a pension by Queen Anne and commissioned to write a *Te Deum* and *Jubilate* to commemorate the Treaty of Utrecht), he stayed on, only to be confronted, as we have seen, by the accession of George I. But any embarrassment this may have caused soon dissipated, and Handel came to enjoy the highest official favour as well as considerable public esteem. His professional life was by no means without vicissitudes, but as a whole it represented a highly successful manipulation of social and financial opportunity. Handel did not reject paid employment; rather, he combined it with risk-bearing enterprise in such a way as to keep himself before the public eye and maximize his gains.

All this would be of little interest were it not for Handel's towering genius. His English contemporaries were given the posts that carried the greatest prestige, but they could not match, even the best of them, the extraordinary vitality of his music. Although English audiences later came to admire Handel for the wrong reasons, there was in many respects an excellent match between their expectations and his propensities. What is more, he found himself well able to adapt his style to changes of taste. It is true that he pursued the cultivation of Italian opera long after realistic hopes that his achievements would be widely appreciated had evaporated. But he was here grappling with a deeper current, and he eventually came to realize that English oratorio, accidentally invented and its artistic potential not immediately grasped, could indeed restore the desired symbiosis between the composer and a wide audience.

The first paragraph of the extract

This is mostly about Handel's employment by Queen Anne and George I of England.

In other words the piece is about the right part of Handel's career (he must have been in London, where Queen Anne and George I lived).

Be selective
Do not note every detail of the passages you read.

Very little else is relevant to Handel's musical evolution. The fact that Handel made money in various sorts of venture in London is not relevant to the question about how his music evolved. It is therefore not necessary to note anything from the first paragraph for this essay.

See pp. 65–7

(There might be other reasons for taking notes from this paragraph. See the section 'How to take notes'.)

The second paragraph of the extract

This makes some very useful statements about whether or not Handel's music developed.

What Caldwell tells us is that it both changed and did not change. He writes, so you note:

Do not forget to write down the page number!

When using quotes you must retain the exact punctuation as it appears in the book in which you found the piece.

> Caldwell, p.2 What is more, he found himself well able to adapt his style to changes of taste. It is true that he pursued the cultivation of Italian opera long after realistic hopes that his achievements would be widely appreciated had evaporated. But he was here grappling with a deeper current, and he eventually came to realize that English oratorio, … could indeed restore the desired symbiosis between the composer and a wide audience.

These three sentences are **all relevant** to your title.

■ The first sentence

> What is more, he found himself well able to adapt his style to changes of taste.

tells us that Handel's music changed when he was in London, since he attempted to keep up with public taste.

> It is true that he pursued the cultivation of Italian opera long after realistic hopes that his achievements would be widely appreciated had evaporated.

informs us Handel's music appeared as though it did not change since he kept on writing Italian-style operas, even after they had gone out of fashion.

■ The third sentence

> But he was here grappling with a deeper current, and he eventually came to realize that English oratorio, ... could indeed restore the desired symbiosis between the composer and a wide audience.

suggests Handel's music was actually changing while he was writing Italian-style operas, since he was using the operas as an experimenting ground for the development of what would become the English oratorio.

When you come to write the essay, you might quote the three sentences together, or separately. It does not matter when you are taking notes. Just make sure you get the words down correctly.

What is important about this information is that it allows you to begin to form an opinion about Handel's London music.

Forming your opinion

From the quotes taken, you might decide that Handel needed money, so he had to write popular music.

■ **Quote 1:** What is more, he found himself well able to adapt his style to changes of taste. (Handel was able to write music that fitted the current fashion.)

Handel's music was popular.

■ **Quote 3:** [Handel]... restore[d] the desired symbiosis between the composer and a wide audience. (Handel wrote music people liked to hear.)

Remember!
Always think while you read. Isaiah Berlin called it 'active reading'. React to what you read, and researching for an essay will be quite fast.

Handel developed a new style of music that would soon become extremely popular.

■ Quote 3: But he was here grappling with a deeper current, and he eventually came to realize that English oratorio, … could indeed restore the desired symbiosis between the composer and a wide audience. (Handel discovered that English oratorio (he wrote *Messiah*) would be popular.)

Against this, the quote taken also shows that Handel continued writing music that was old-fashioned

■ Quote 2: It is true that he pursued the cultivation of Italian opera long after realistic hopes that his achievements would be widely appreciated had evaporated (Handel continued to write music that was out of fashion.)

You have now the **evidence** for an **opinion**. At present, the balance of evidence is that Handel's music did change while he was in London.

After reading five other versions about Handel's time in London, you might have a different opinion, but this is why you do research: to find **evidence** on which to base your **opinion**, which will be the motivation for your essay.

Developing the argument

Remember!
Write more about less.

An important difference in essay writing between undergraduate level and school or access course is that at the higher level you are graded more on your ability to make a **coherent argument**, and less on the amount of information presented.

The way to think about it is to remember that in all the essays you have written so far, you have had to say a little bit about a lot of information.

In an undergraduate essay, you need to say a lot about a little bit of information.

Do not write a long list of facts about your topic. You have to say something interesting about five or six facts.

To do this, you have to focus in on the facts in great detail, so that you can arrange the facts into an argument.

What am I trying to argue?

This is where you can go back to your translation of the question. For example, you might 'translate' the following essay question:

■ How great was the influence of women on the development of the novel in the eighteenth century?

into, say:

■ How great was the influence of my favourite singer on the music of the early twenty-first century?

Now let us explore the different ways you can argue.

Types of argument

When you have decided what the question is asking, and you have done your research, write out a brief answer in about 100 words.

An answer to the example question in its translated form might go something like:

I think my favourite singer contributed greatly to recent developments in music. I would emphasize three key points. First, her songs have been re-recorded by more than twenty other popular musicians; second, her music is to be heard daily on the radio; third, her tours sell out hours after they are announced. Having said that, however, I think that it is fair to say that the second and third points are also applicable to several other singers and pop bands who have one hit song that is quickly forgotten. So all things considered, I think it might be best to argue that my favourite singer's influence was limited to just the first of my original three points.

31

Another answer to the same question, which would lead from different evidence, might be:

> My favourite singer played no part in the recent developments in music. Latest research shows that popular music is entirely conditioned by the colour of shirts young people wear, and not by listening to the music made by other musicians. This has been shown to be the case by Professor Joao Bloggs in the book *Shirt colour and the writing of pop songs*. Of course I, like everyone else, instinctively feel that other contemporary music does influence developments in the form. But the scientific evidence to the contrary compels me to conclude that this feeling is misleading, and that shirt colour alone is the influence on contemporary popular musicians.

- ■ What makes these answers good is that they are made up from coherent arguments, and based on acceptable evidence.

- ■ Degree essays are not looking for a right or wrong answer, but a good argument either way.

By contrast, the following is a bad answer to the same question.

> In order to answer the question, I shall tell you something about my favourite singer. She is Canadian, born of Caucasian and native American parents. She began to write songs while at school in Michigan, and played in folk clubs while she was at university. At one club in Chicago she was heard by a talent scout who signed her up to A&B records. The main influences on her music were native American music, jazz and folk music, and we can hear these three strands clearly throughout her oeuvre. Her most commercially successful album was *Music is the colour of my shirt*, which sold 5 million copies. Thus we can be sure that her music influenced many musicians of the early twenty-first century.

Note
Evidence must give grounds for your reader to accept your opinion.

What makes the bad answer unsatisfactory is not that the facts are wrong—there are lots of them, and they are presumably correct—but that the conclusion does not lead from the evidence, and so there is no coherent argument.

The facts about the musician's life, even the popularity of one album, do not demonstrate an influence on any other musicians. The facts may be correct but they are irrelevant to the question.

What should I argue?

There is no right answer that will guarantee you high marks. You will be graded on the **coherence** of your argument, not on whether you agree with the examiner.

But however coherent your argument, your essay will not work if it is not easy to read. There are two elements to making your essay an easy read: the structure of the essay and the clarity of your language. These topics will be covered in the next two chapters.

4 Structuring the essay

The decision about what information goes where in an essay can be complicated. Based on what you have learned so far, you can make these decisions much more easily.

You are writing an essay in order to give your **opinion** about something, so first:

■ Introduce your opinion and your reasons for holding it.

You must offer **evidence** as to why your opinion is valid, so next present:

■ evidence for your opinion.

Finally you must show the **scope** of your opinion, and how it fits with other opinions, so:

■ Conclude your essay with a look at other people's ideas to show how your opinion fits with theirs.

Parts of an essay

An essay is only as good as its introduction. An introduction must be followed by a number of pieces of evidence (the 'body of the essay'). The evidence must lead to the conclusion.

This chapter will therefore be presented under three sub-headings:

■ introduction;

■ body of the essay;

■ conclusion.

Introduction

Getting the opening statement right is perhaps the most important factor in the essay-writing process. You need to say three things:

- what you are going to write about;

- which sources you will call upon to support your argument;

- a brief statement of what you hope to demonstrate.

It is always tempting to hold back your conclusions at this point so you can end with a triumphant statement of what you have done. **Do not hold anything back**.

A metaphor for introductions

Pull the rabbit out of the hat right at the beginning. Show your reader the rabbit, so you can spend the rest of the essay describing your 'common burrowing rodent'.

Focus

What you are trying to do when you write the introduction is to focus in on the little bit of information about which you are going to argue an opinion. So your reader will need to:

- know what you are going to write about;

- know which sources you will call upon to support your argument;

- read a brief statement of what you hope to demonstrate.

Try to use the word 'demonstrate'. You are not going to **prove** anything, you are going to demonstrate that your argument is not out of the question.

Think about your reader

There is nothing more frustrating than trying to understand why this or that little piece of information has been mentioned in an essay without first knowing where the argument is going.

Sell yourself

You wouldn't buy, say, a car or a computer without first finding out about its specifications. You need to know what it can do *before* you shell out your hard-earned cash.

Imagine that the introduction is the advertising brochure for your essay. In it you must give all the information that will help your reader to buy your argument.

The brochure, like the introduction, is not the argument itself, but must say what the argument is going to be, and why it is a good argument. **The introduction must say why the argument is worth believing**.

What should not go into an introduction

There is no space for a general statement about the whole topic before you get going on the nitty-gritty.

Imagine a brochure for a sports car that started with a history of the first hundred years of the automobile. You would think to yourself: I don't need to know this. I want to know about the sports car I have my eye on.

Wording the introduction

While writing your introduction, keep in your mind the words:

■ 'This essay will argue that …'

In this way you will quickly focus in on what you have to say and avoid irrelevance.

How long should the introduction be?

Take time on the introduction. You should mention all the ins and outs of the argument.

Not that the story needs to be long, but it will take a long while to make it short.

(Thoreau)

Base it on the 100-word outline arguments you saw in the 'Developing the argument' section above.

Remember that you can argue **for** or **against** the statement in the question. You can even argue both for **and** against the statement in the question, so long as you say why you think both are true. And it is the introduction where you should say this.

Your introduction can be as long as 500 or 600 words in a 2,000-word essay and should make up one paragraph.

The body of the essay

If you have written a good introduction, the main part of your essay will not be so hard. It will fill in the details of the brochure you laid out in the introduction.

What each paragraph should contain

To make sure you remain relevant throughout your essay, each paragraph of the body of your essay should:

- present some evidence;

- say where the evidence came from (**context**);

- say why that evidence is part of the argument (**comment**).

What is evidence?

The evidence in each paragraph is the outcome of your research. It could be:

- in the form of a quotation from a book;

- data from an experiment;

- from observations of some other type.

Some circumstantial evidence is very strong, as when you find a trout in the milk.
(Thoreau)

37

Presenting evidence

Both **context** and **comment** are necessary for your argument. There is no point in giving evidence without saying why it fits into your argument. Nor is there any point in repeating your argument without giving evidence to support it.

Thus, each paragraph of your essay will be quite similar. Each will give contextualized evidence and weave that evidence into the cloth of the argument.

Keep on adding paragraphs until enough evidence is given for the argument to be deemed worthwhile. I would say five or six pieces of evidence are enough for a 2,000-word essay.

Example paragraph

Here is an example of a paragraph from the essay 'How far did Handel's music evolve during his time in London?' based on the notes taken above. Each paragraph of the body of your essay should read something like this, evidence followed by comment:

We find a complex statement about Handel's musical development in John Caldwell's *Oxford History of English Music*. Caldwell writes of Handel's period in London:

> It is true that he [Handel] pursued the cultivation of Italian opera long after realistic hopes that his achievements would be widely appreciated had evaporated. But he was here grappling with a deeper current, and he eventually came to realize that English oratorio, ... could indeed restore the desired symbiosis between the composer and a wide audience.

Note that following the quotation is a restatement of what Caldwell says, but in different words. It is important always to rewrite quotes so your reader can understand what the quote means for you and your argument.

In this statement, Caldwell accounts for Handel's continued output of Italian operas long after their fall from popularity. He suggests that the composer was using the opera as a testing ground for new ideas about music, which would become the English oratorio. In terms of the question of the evolution of Handel's music during his residence in London, we might therefore argue that superficially Handel's music remained unchanged. He continued to write in modes, such as the Italian opera, which were outdated. However, it would also seem true to argue that Handel's music was evolving even at this time, since traits that would become familiar in the English oratorio are clearly discernible in the later Italian operas.

How many paragraphs should I write?

This example paragraph is about 200 words long. Six like it will give a word count of about 1,200 words, and with the introduction and conclusion, you will have a 2,000-word essay.

How different should each paragraph be?

It is tempting, when you get to the body of your essay, to begin a new argument in each paragraph. You might think that you are giving a different angle on the problem, which will highlight the problem in an interesting way.

This is not the case.

This method clouds the issue, so that your reader will wonder what is being argued in the whole piece. By starting on a new argument in each paragraph, what you are doing is writing six (or more) 'essaylets' rather than presenting a coherent argument. Each piece of evidence should be used to support **one** argument.

Conclusion

The conclusion is the easiest part of an essay. It should restate that the preceding argument is valid, and why. In other words it should repeat the introduction, though it should be briefer.

The conclusion is also the hardest part of the essay. In addition to restating the argument, you need to point out where your argument stands with respect to other ideas about the same topic.

Remember, you are not trying to say everything there is to say about your topic. You are trying to write an essay, and ...

An essay is your opinion about a little bit of a subject, in which you use evidence to support your opinion.

What should go in the conclusion

The conclusion is where you can bring in any other research you carried out, but did not quote in the body of your essay since it was not relevant to your argument.

In the conclusion you can state that your essay does not agree with the argument in this or that book, and explain why.

Then you must say why you think your argument is better, or maybe equally good. Once again, you cannot deal with all the other arguments there are; choose one or two, and stop after 200 or 300 words. Again, the conclusion should make up one paragraph.

What should not go in the conclusion

Take extra care in your conclusion that you do not say anything that you have not made an argument for in the rest of the essay.

Do not draw general conclusions from your evidence.

If, for instance, you have been writing an essay 'How important is the factor of impact in marketing communications?' you will have given evidence from, say, one or two marketing campaigns.

However, just because a particular strategy has been successfully employed in these cases does not mean that the strategies are infallible.

Imagine, if all advertising slogans were almost the same: 'Eat … it tastes sooo good.'; 'Drink … it tastes sooo good.' The impact would sooon fade away.

You can conclude with some certainty that the campaigns you chose were successful or unsuccessful because of the strategies used.

You cannot conclude that all campaigns which use the successful strategy will be successful, nor that an unsuccessful strategy will not bear fruit in other circumstances.

So remember, draw your conclusions only from the evidence you have presented. You have not solved all the problems of the topic, so do not claim you have. Leave other options open: such as the fact that you might be wrong.

5 Getting the words in the right order

Clear writers,
like fountains, do
not seem so deep
as they are; the
turbid look the
most profound.

(Landor)

Words and sentences are the building blocks of the essay. Which words you choose and how they are put together into sentences can either make your argument clear or render it incomprehensible.

■ The right choice of word is the key to **clarity** in an essay.

■ **Brevity** is the key to writing clear sentences.

But first of all you must simply get down on paper what you want to say.

Drafting

No essay can be written perfectly at one go. You will need to write a series of drafts (at least two), to make sure you are as clear as you can be.

The first draft

When you have chosen your essay title, done your research, and sketched out your argument, choose six of the best quotes and write down what you want to argue in each paragraph as quickly as you can.

Start with each of the six quotes, and write down quickly why you think it can be used as evidence for your opinion. There is no need to try to make well-formed sentences; just get the ideas down on paper. This process will form the basis for each paragraph.

Read this draft through, and decide which paragraphs you think will be the most relevant. These will be the ones that most nearly agree with each other, and with your opinion.

Do not be afraid to discard paragraphs that do not fit with the others. If you need to find other quotes, on which to base new paragraphs, check through your research notes first. After writing your first draft you might discover that a quote that you did not think relevant has become important. Only go back to the books if you are really short of material.

The second draft

When you are satisfied that you have six quotes and six basic paragraphs that all go together to present evidence for your opinion, take a coffee break. You need to rewrite them in proper sentences, and in language that is as clear and readable as possible. So come to this stage of writing as fresh and alert as you can.

What you are trying to do is to link your ideas together into a logical argument. So you need to be able to see how a paragraph fits together. If we go back to the sample paragraph, we can break it down into sections:

> We find a complex statement about Handel's musical development in John Caldwell's *Oxford History of English Music*. Caldwell writes of Handel's period in London:

■ This sentence introduces the quotation and states that it is relevant to the question.

It is followed by the quotation itself, your evidence:

> It is true that he [Handel] pursued the cultivation of Italian opera long after realistic hopes that his achievements would be widely appreciated had evaporated. But he was here grappling with a deeper current, and he eventually came to realize that English oratorio, ... could indeed restore the desired symbiosis between the composer and a wide audience.

5 Getting the words in the right order

*Then, rising
with Aurora's
light, The Muse
invoked, sit down
to write; Blot out,
correct, insert,
refine, Enlarge,
diminish,
interline.*

(Swift)

Stages in drafting

1. FIRST DRAFT
Get your initial ideas down on paper.

2. SECOND DRAFT
Rewrite the ideas in proper linked sentences.

Next, it is important to let your reader know what the quote means:

> In this statement, Caldwell accounts for Handel's continued output of Italian operas long after their fall from popularity. He suggests that the composer was using the opera as a testing ground for new ideas about music, which would become the English oratorio.

■ These sentences give a brief translation of the quotation.

It is very important **not** to leave a quote to stand by itself. You must say what it means to you. Other readers might think it means something entirely different.

Here the explanation is introduced with the phrase 'In this statement'. You might use other phrases such as 'In other words ...', or 'By this we might understand ...'.

Following the explanation, you need to show how the evidence fits with your opinion:

> In terms of the question of the evolution of Handel's music during his residence in London, we might therefore argue that superficially Handel's music remained unchanged.

■ The beginning of this sentence refers the reader back to the terms of the question.

■ The end of the sentence shows what evidence the quotation brings to the question.

This type of sentence is crucial to an essay. It employs both the terms of the question and the evidence quoted. It is the pivotal point at which the two meet. Try always to bring in some sort of version of this sentence. It will make sure that you are answering the question. Furthermore, it will make your argument clear, since it contains both the terms of the question and the answer you are giving. But once you have given your answer, draw attention to the specifics of the evidence you have presented.

> He continued to write in modes, such as the Italian opera, which were outdated.

Using quotes

Remember to explain what a quote means to you; interpret it for your readers.

■ This sentence moves from general information to specific information.

While the pivotal sentence tells us that Handel's music did not change, this sentence tells us what evidence there is for holding your opinion: that he continued to write in an outmoded style—that of Italian opera.

It might be introduced simply as in the example, or with words that suggest the inevitability of holding the view, such as:

■ Thus, ...

■ Therefore, ...

The sample sentence might be reworded:

Thus, he continued to write in modes, such as the Italian opera, which were outdated.

Or

Therefore we can see that Handel continued to write in modes, such as the Italian opera, which were outdated.

Although the information is there in the quotation, you must draw your reader's attention to it. You might feel you are pushing your point home too strongly, but it will make your essay clear. Your reader needs to know what *you* make of the evidence.

However, not all information gives facts in a simple way, so you must learn to nuance your essay with modifiers:

However, it would also seem true to argue that Handel's music was evolving even at this time, since traits that would become familiar in the English oratorio are clearly discernible in the later Italian operas.

It's important to put your point across in a striking way.

■ This sentence modifies the simple claim of the first part of the paragraph.

5 Getting the words in the right order

Nuances are very important in essays. They might be introduced by words such as:

- Nevertheless
- Although
- Furthermore
- Still
- But
- However

Caution!

To nuance your argument can also look dithering. Remember that your argument should always be clear, and that nuances are simply added to show there may be other ways of interpreting the evidence you present.

See pp. 72–3 for more information on short sentences.

Handel did not simply write outmoded Italian operas; at the same time he was developing his musical style into what would become the English oratorio. The word 'However' introduces this modification, and nuances the argument from the simple statement that Handel's work did not progress to one which claims that it progressed in an undercover way.

Nuances such as this are extremely important: this is the meat and drink of essay writing. No argument is cut and dried, and it is the number of nuances that you can introduce that will show your reader how much you know about a subject.

When you redraft your paragraphs it is a good idea to bring in nuancing words to introduce the different ways of seeing the same piece of evidence. It is here that you show yourself thinking, so it is here that you must be clear.

Word choices

Always try to use a simple word accurately. Bringing in long words can obfuscate your meaning (make it less clear).

If you use a **new** or **unfamiliar word** that you have learned in your lectures, reading, or in seminars, add a short account of what it means to you. Then your reader can be sure what you are saying.

Sentence length

When you are redrafting try to keep the length of your sentences to a medium of fifteen words.

Word count

Your institution will set a word length on all your undergraduate essays. It might be 2,000 (the most common) or perhaps 3,500 words.

What is included in the word count?

Regulations vary, but the word count usually excludes quotations from other sources and supplementary material such as notes and bibliographies. Regulations do not vary when it comes to overshooting or undershooting word counts.

How much can my word count vary?

For a 2,000-word essay, anything in the range of 1,800 to 2,200 words (excluding quotes, notes, and bibliography) will count as 2,000 words. If you write more, you will be marked down. If you write less, you will also be marked down.

Why stick to the word count?

One skill you are learning is precision. You have to be able to say everything that needs saying in the required number of words. So you have to pare down to the barest minimum. There is no room for waffle.

If your word count is too short, you will be marked down for writing too little because you look lazy.

Top tip!
Always keep to your word count. You should be able to say what you need to concisely and convincingly in the allotted number of words.

6 | Presentation

Now you have finished writing.

You have:

■ chosen your title;

■ done your research;

■ found your quotes;

■ chosen the right words;

■ put them in the right order.

It is tempting to do a word count to make sure you have not over- or undershot your target, so you can hand in your essay ahead of the deadline. But however good your ideas, handing in four sheets of scrawl will not make a good impression.

Word-processing

Nowadays, it is best to word-process your essay. Most institutions provide inexpensive facilities for under-graduates to type out and print essays.

Why should I word-process?

You may find that your institution does not require that your work is word-processed in the first year as an undergraduate. However, you *will* find that **some** of your work (probably your dissertation) **must** be word-processed.

One Last Lap

Paying someone to type for you is expensive, so it is an idea to learn how to type. If you do not have a computer of your own, find out how to gain access to your institution's network, and how to use it.

Universities and colleges usually hold regular word-processing courses. Sign on to one as soon as you can. These courses are usually provided free.

It is also a good idea to learn word-processing since it is a 'transferable skill'. It is becoming a requirement for many types of job.

How your essay should look

Page layout

You are aiming to differentiate between the types of information on the page. These will be:

- the information about the essay:
  the title;
  your name;
  the name of the module being assessed.

- the essay proper:
  your own ideas.

- quotes, pictures, and diagrams:
  other people's material.

General comments on page layout

The first thing to remember about the whole essay is always to **double-space**. That is, leave a blank line between each line you write.

If you are writing by hand, miss a line each line. If you are word-processing, the computer will do it for you. It is important that your work is easy to read.

Double spacing

Double-spaced work allows your marker to see your work clearly and to write comments in between lines.

Margins

Leave two-inch margins on either side of your page for the same reason.

Font size, writing size

Choose an appropriately large font (say, 12 point) or use hand-writing that is bigger and neater than normal.

If you hand in an illegibly written essay you will be marked down, and might be asked to come in and read it out loud to your tutor. The process is very embarrassing for all concerned.

The power of the visual

Make your essay a pleasure to look at and it will be a pleasure to read.

Write on one side of the paper

It ensures your work is legible.

At the top of the first page

- Start with the title in a large font (say, 14 point) and in **bold type**. If you are writing by hand, underline it.

- In smaller font (say, 12 point) but still in **bold type**, put your name and student identification code.

- Next line, same size font, still in **bold type**, put the number of the module and the module title.

- Leave a line (which will automatically be two lines in double spacing).

- Now write your essay in a good size font (say, 12 point), Roman type, not in *italics*, and not in **bold type**.

Your first page should look something like this:

To what extent can it be argued that Byron and Keats are second-generation Romantic poets?

14pt bold type

Joe Bloggs Student no. 99004521

12pt bold type

EL 2534: The Beauties of Poetry 1750-1850.

12pt bold type

line spacing

This essay will argue that despite the fact that Keats idolized Byron's poetry, and used it as a model for his own, both poets can be described, with some reservations, as second-generation Romantic poets. Byron, who antedated Keats, could be thought of as a first-generation Romantic poet. However, this essay will demonstrate that his themes and techniques clearly place him in the second generation. Reference here will be made to Byron's *Hours of Idleness* (1807), which contains a number of translations and imitations of classical authors.

12pt Roman type

| ## Quotations

There are two main ways of marking quotations.

Short prose quotations

For prose quotes under, say, fifteen words, use quotation marks within the text.

Long prose quotatations

For prose quotations of more than fifteen words, indent them in a separate block paragraph, and **do not use quotation marks**.

Examples

The different quotes should look like this:

Notice the use of '[*sic*]' (the Latin for 'thus') after the first use of the word 'Generall'. This indicates that the word is spelled this way by Defoe. You only have to make the note once.

> ... and at this point, we notice that where Defoe writes, "and Chang'd the Generall [*sic*]", George Harris Healey notes that
>
>> The incompetent Duke of Schomberg, commanding British troops in Portugal, had just been relieved in favour of the Earl of Galway.
>
> From the informal way Defoe refers to Schomberg, as "the Generall", we can see the close relationship between Defoe and the Earl of Oxford ... .

Poetry quotations

When you quote poetry, always quote it in an indented block (however few the words), and in the lines in which it was written, even if you are starting from the middle of a line.

All quotes from poetry should look like this:

... although from the same sonnet we can see what might be thought of as Wordsworth's concern with the air quality of London:

> ... fields, towers and temples lie,
> Open unto the fields and to the sky
> All bright and glistening in the smokeless air.

This is all well and good from a twentieth-century perspective. However, the argument is less easy to make in the light of statements that emanate from critics such as ...

Illustrations etc.

Any visual material, such as graphs, diagrams, or pictures, must be given a wide margin, and separated from the written text.

Remember to number this material and to give a title for each illustration or graph, etc., even if it is obvious what it is from the surrounding text.

Source notes and bibliography

It is vital to avoid a charge of plagiarism when you are writing an essay. That is to say, you must always make it clear which ideas are yours and when you are quoting someone else's work.

The page layout suggested above and the use of double quotation marks will go a certain way towards achieving this. However, in a degree essay, you must always note or reference quotes and supply a bibliography of the books you have read.

Wherever you have quoted someone else in their own words, **or even if you have paraphrased someone else's idea**, reference the source using a superscript number (a number above the line of the text, like this,[3]) and write down the details of the source at the bottom of the page.

Students are endlessly admonished to avoid plagiarism nowadays, so much so that they feel they should know what it is and daren't ask. Plagiarism is putting your name to work that was done by someone else.

The form your notes should take should be given in your institution's STYLE SHEET. If you cannot obtain this, your note should contain the following information, and in this order:

■ author or editor: full name, first name first;

■ *title: full title of book, including subtitle, in italics*;

■ translator (if any);

■ edition number (if it is not the first edition);

■ number of volumes (if it is a multi-volume work);

■ volume number from which the quote is taken;

■ facts of publication: (city: publisher, date);

■ page number.

See pp.112–21 for more details on notes and bibliography.

When you have finished your essay write the list of books cited at the end. This will be your bibliography.

You will find further details of how to make citations from various different types of source in Part B.

Print and edit

Spotting errors

Always read your essay through at least once in its printed form.

Reading from the screen can lead to errors. When you have finished your essay, complete with all the notes and bibliography, print it out **and read it through again**.

Read with a coloured pencil in one hand, and mark:

■ places where your argument seems weak;

■ badly worded sentences;

■ mistakes in page layout
  ○ no quotation marks around indented quotes;
  ○ 'widows' (where the last word or line of a paragraph appears at the top of a page) and 'orphans' (where the first line of a paragraph appears at the bottom of a page);
  ○ italicized or emboldened words that need to be in roman type;

- spelling mistakes;

- punctuation.

You will find a section on common errors in spelling and punctuation in Part B.

When you have marked any errors or things you do not like, make changes on this rough copy, then transfer the changes to the word-processor.

Now put in the **page numbers**.

Handwritten essays

If you are handwriting an essay, you should edit at least one copy. The version you hand in should have **no crossings out**. You should also number the pages.

Presentation

The visual impression an essay makes should suggest its high quality. It is a good idea to cover your essay with a temporary binder. These are available at most stationery shops, and can be used over and over again.

Make sure the binder you choose enables the essay to be opened and read easily.

When you have put your essay in the binder, read through it quickly to make sure:

- the pages are in the right order;

- all the pages are there.

How can you contrive to write so even?

(Austen)

Tip
At the very least you must staple your essay together. DO NOT HAND IT IN FASTENED WITH A PAPERCLIP—pages will be lost.

7 Managing your time

However good an essay is, you must hand it in on time, otherwise your institution will impose marking penalties. This is because if you have more time than other students to write your essay, it is as though you have been allowed to continue writing after the end of an exam.

To meet deadlines you have to plan your work carefully.

Full-time students

Most full-time degrees are made up of four 'courses' or 'modules' per term or semester, with one essay and one exam per module.

- Essay hand-in dates usually come at the middle and the end of a teaching period.
- Exams are usually sat during an assessment period at the end of each term or semester, or at the end of the year.

It is vital you arrange to write essays well before the deadline, so you do not find yourself trying to research and write two essays in a single week.

Part-time students

If you are doing your degree part-time, you will probably do half the number of modules a term or semester. You may be entitled to do only one if you want to do your degree more slowly.

Because you will have less time to research and write, double the number of weeks spent on each element of producing an essay: researching and writing.

Your assignment schedule

The first thing to do in planning your writing and research is to draw a schedule of your term or semester showing the dates when the essays are to be handed in. Here is a sample timetable based on four modules (A to D).

If you have semesters, your essay schedule might look something like this:

Week 1:
Week 2:
Week 3:
Week 4:
Week 5:
Week 6:
Week 7:
Week 8: Essays A and B
Week 9:
Week 10:
Week 11:
Week 12:
Week 13:
Week 14:
Week 15: Essays C and D

If you work in terms, your essay schedule might look something like this:

Week 1:
Week 2:
Week 3:
Week 4: Essay A
Week 5:
Week 6: Essay B
Week 7 :
Week 8: Essay C
Week 9:
Week 10: Essay D

At this point your essays will either look a long way off, or like a row of hurdles to jump that are looming very large. Neither view is very helpful. Your essay deadlines are nearer than you think, but there is enough time to research and write them.

It was suggested in the earlier part of the book that you read around your subject for a few weeks before choosing which essay to do. Get into the habit of working at fixed times during the week. Arrange four three-hour sessions researching in the library. These can become slots for researching and writing

Three hours a day will produce as much as a man ought to write.
(Trollope)

your essays later on. But when you start working for essays, do not forget that you will also have to carry on doing your weekly reading for lectures and seminars.

Your weekly timetable

It is best to work out a weekly timetable in which you put enough library time to read for your courses, as well as research and write your essays. Here is a sample timetable based on four modules (A to D) taught in four sessions.

	a.m.	p.m.
Monday	Teaching A	
Tuesday		Teaching B
Wednesday	Teaching C	
Thursday		
Friday		Teaching D

Add to this your reading sessions, trying to place the reading times before the teaching sessions. You may have more teaching sessions for your modules, though the sessions will be shorter. If you are taught this way, put in more, shorter reading sessions.

	a.m.	p.m.
Monday	Teaching A	Reading B
Tuesday	Reading C	Teaching B
Wednesday	Teaching C	
Thursday	Reading A	
Friday	Reading D	Teaching D

Wednesday afternoons are almost universally kept for sports, so there will be little or no teaching. It is also the time for clubs to meet, so try to keep it free. Keep some time to yourself and your friends, especially the weekends, and perhaps try to keep the evenings free as well. There is no point going on working all the hours the library is open. You will stop 'listening to' what you are reading.

With this weekly guide you have one afternoon to catch up on things you might not have been able to fit in. It is a good idea to keep some spare work time like this for emergencies.

When you have worked out your weekly timetable with your reading times, go back to your assignment schedule and fill in the weeks in which you need to research and write your essays.

Researching and writing schedule

You probably need two sessions researching and two sessions writing each essay. Since you will still be reading for each week, you will need to find time for two sessions a week for researching or writing since you must continue to read for your modules.

If you have semesters, your schedule might look something like this:

Week 1:
Week 2:
Week 3:
Week 4:
Week 5: Research A
Week 6: Write A
Week 7: Research B
Week 8: Write B
Week 9:
Week 10:
Week 11:
Week 12: Research C
Week 13: Write C
Week 14: Research D
Week 15: Write D

If you work in terms, your schedule might look something like this:

Week 1:
Week 2:
Week 3: Research A
Week 4: Write A
Week 5: Research B
Week 6: Write B
Week 7 : Research C
Week 8: Write C
Week 9: Research D
Week 10: Write D

You will have either to cut down the time you read for your modules or to add extra sessions to your workload. Since you already have one afternoon for emergencies, this might be the time for one extra session to use for researching and writing. You might therefore add another session one evening.

There is no hard and fast guide to researching and writing essays. You must adapt this example to how quickly you work, and to the times you are free, depending upon your commitments.

Essay extensions

There are sometimes good reasons why you might miss an essay deadline. You might have the 'flu, or there may be a family crisis.

In these circumstances you need a bit of foresight, but act **before** the deadline wherever possible.

What you need if you are going to be late with an essay is more time, usually called an 'extension'. Most institutions will offer you these if you have good reason. They represent a new agreed deadline.

Commonly, you must

■ fill in a form;

and present an

■ official document

which states why your request should be considered. Such documents might be from:
- your GP (if you are ill);
- from the police (if you have, say, been involved in an accident);
- your institution's counselling service (if there is a family crisis).

It is important to get the extension **before** the deadline.

If you are ill and cannot get in to fill in the form, telephone, email, or fax your institution and explain the details.

If you need to see the counselling service, make sure you get an appointment as quickly as possible.

Disabilities

If you have a learning disability, or some other notifiable condition which might affect **all** of your essay deadlines, such as dyslexia, non-verbal learning disability syndrome, bipolar disorder, or Asperger's syndrome, you may inform your institution when you begin your degree and a convenient package of extensions will be worked out that will suit you best throughout your degree.

If you are ill let your institution know that you require an essay extension.

It is up to you to tell them. If you do not want special treatment, you do not have to have it. No one will ask you and you do not have to tell.

Emergencies

If something happens the day before handing in an essay, which means you cannot put the finishing touches to it, hand in the work that you have done.

Perhaps you can:

- get someone else to hand it in for you;

- email or fax it to your department office.

Make sure you enclose a note saying what has happened and asking whether you can arrange an extension at short notice, or after the fact.

8 More about research

Chapter 3 suggested two ways of finding books to build up your own bibliography, and how to read to find quotations to use in an essay. This chapter offers a few more ways of finding information on the topic of your essay, and some more thoughts on taking notes.

Finding books

There are three further methods for gathering information described here:

■ author search;

■ bibliography search;

■ Internet search.

Author search

If your library has a computer catalogue, select the function AUTHOR SEARCH. If someone has published a book on a topic, they often publish another.

1. Enter the name of an author from the module bibliography.

2. Take the shelf mark of any other books the author has written, and find the book.

This search method will produce only a few books. However, you can use just one book on a subject to find many more. You can do this by using a BIBLIOGRAPHY SEARCH.

Bibliography searches

Find any book on a subject close to that of your essay (perhaps one you have found in the author search). Turn to the back and you will almost certainly find a BIBLIOGRAPHY. It may be called a LIST of WORKS CITED.

This will be the list of books the author read to write the book. These books will therefore be relevant to your topic as well. Check if you have any of them in your library.

Internet searches

One final way to get a list of books on a particular topic is to search on the Internet. You need to start with a good search engine, such as Yahoo, Manjara, or Google.

The search engine most in use is Google. It is especially good as it searches the content of websites, not just their titles.

1. Enter the web address (http://www.google.com).

2. Enter any number of words you think might help.

3. You can put in as many words as you want to narrow down the search.

4. You will get many, many results.

Example

A Google search on 'Renaissance courts' found 62,000 sites. A similar search on 'physical geography' came up with 581,000 sites.

Selected Bibliography

The following reference books have either proved invaluable in the writing of this dictionary or are recommended by the authors. An additional list includes key periodicals and magazines.

Anderson, Jack, *Dance* (New York: Newsweek, 1974).

—— *The World of Modern Dance: Art without Boundaries* (Iowa City: University of Iowa Press, 1997).

Au, Susan, *Ballet and Modern Dance* (London: Thames and Hudson, 1988).

Balanchine, George, and Mason, Francis, *Balanchine's Festival of Ballet*, i and ii (London: W. H. Allen, 1978); originally published as *Balanchine's Complete Stories of the Great Ballets* (Garden City, NY: Doubleday, 1954).

Banes, Sally, *Terpsichore in Sneakers: Post-Modern Dance* (Middletown, Conn.: Wesleyan University Press, 1987).

An extract from a bibliography to a published book is shown above.

You will find urls (web addresses) for other search engines in the Resource List on pages 122–3.

What you have found is a list of all the sites in the world that contain the words you have entered.

Although it may seem there are far too many sites to go through, you will not have to look through more than two or three pages.

■ Search for sites with the suffix '.ac.uk' or '.edu'.

These are sites of British and American academic institutions, and many publish their bibliographies on the web.

■ Click on the site and look for the lists of modules run by these institutions.

■ Look for the module with the name most similar to yours.

■ Look for the bibliography from that module and you may find a title that will suit you, which is available in your library.

Two warnings about using the Internet

Remember, what you are surfing the Web for is the titles of books. If you find an essay on the Internet that is roughly on the same topic as the one you are to write on, **think**: if you can find it, so can your lecturer. Handing in someone else's work might seem the easy road to glory, but it is stealing. If you are found out, you will be thrown out of your institution with no qualification.

Remember, too, that some people think it is fun to get you into this kind of trouble. There is an essay on the Net that says it is about the novel *Gulliver's Travels*, but the writer has changed all the names of the characters in the novel, and has these characters quoting from Dickens—who wrote a hundred years later. The student handing in this essay, which was found on the Net, was caught red-handed.

How to take notes

Chapter 3 suggested that you found and wrote down quotes when reading a book. This is good discipline. It is annoying to have to go back to a book and try to remember the page if you failed to write down a quote accurately, or forgot to note the page number.

Nevertheless, you might find some information that is not really relevant to your essay, but that might be useful for other purposes, even for forthcoming exams. What you might do in this case would be to jot down a few words that will remind you of the idea, without writing down the whole sentence.

What you will need to do is:

- write down the point as accurately as possible;

- copy down any words you might be unfamiliar with;

- make the note as short as possible, but take it in a form that is going to be useful later.

(Note-taking is a complex issue, and will be examined in more detail in another book in this series on *Study Skills*.)

Handel in London
1714 :
• time of Treaty of Utrecht
• soon after death of Queen Anne
• beginning of Hanoverian dynasty

A useful tip about taking notes

If you want to put pencil or pen marks on a passage you are reading, photocopy it first. This is a good way of reading and noting—you might like to highlight words and phrases that could be useful in future. Only people worse than book hogs put marks in library books.

When to stop taking notes

By the time you have about **six** sides of notes and quotes you probably have enough evidence for an undergraduate essay.

Stop taking notes now even if there are more books on your pile. Even if you have not read through all the books you thought might be relevant, stop reading.

Remember!
An essay is about a little bit of a subject ... Too much information is as bad as too little in an undergraduate essay.

65

Remember that you only have to write your essay about a little bit of a subject. You do not have to read from the beginning, right through a book.

Always be selective in what you read.

It may seem a pity to waste the time you have spent on finding the book when the information might be useful as background information. However, beware that background information does not overshadow the task in hand.

When you are reading, it is a good idea from time to time to follow up on leads that might be useful for your essay. Let us look once again at the paragraph about Handel which we did not think relevant for note-taking in Chapter 3:

Select only the essential material from your sources for use in your essay.

The career of Handel in England in many ways anticipates that of a composer such as Mozart in youth or Haydn in his later years in its jettisoning of the constraints of service for the sake of independence and the risks and rewards of catering for the public taste. In this respect Handel's own predilections coincided with the imperatives of English musical life, where the social and political structure did not allow of congenial long-term employment outside the increasingly humdrum routine of the royal court and chapel and that of the major churches. Handel had experienced a mixture of enterprise and short-term employment (with the marquis Francesco Ruspoli) in Italy, and had subsequently become Kapellmeister to the elector of Hanover, later George I of England. On his first visit to England Handel achieved enormous musical and social success, and this must have encouraged him to return, ostensibly for a second short visit, in 1712. Encouraged by his ready acceptance (he was given a pension by Queen Anne and commissioned to write a *Te Deum* and *Jubilate* to commemorate the Treaty of Utrecht), he stayed on, only to be confronted, as we have seen, by the accession of George I. But any embarrassment this may have caused soon dissipated, and Handel came to enjoy the highest official favour as well as considerable public esteem. His professional life was by no means without vicissitudes, but as a whole it represented a highly successful manipulation of social and financial opportunity. Handel did not reject paid employment; rather, he combined it with risk-bearing enterprise in such a way as to keep himself before the public eye and maximize his gains.

Following 'trails'

We first read: 'The career of Handel in England in many ways antici-pates that of a composer such as Mozart in youth or Haydn in his later years.' This means that the author of the piece believes Handel's career anticipated that of Mozart and Haydn. It might be useful to follow this trail and find out more about Handel in books about these other composers. You might search for books on Mozart and Haydn, and check for references to Handel in the **contents page** or **index**. If there is nothing, do not look for evidence in the rest of the book. Put it to one side.

Next, we read how 'the social and political structure' may have influenced Handel's music at the time. It might be a good idea to look at history books about the period, which are not primarily concerned with music. Once again check the **contents page** and **index** for references to the music of the period, or even to references to the Treaty of Utrecht, which is also mentioned in the paragraph.

John Caldwell: The Oxford History of English Music, Vol. 2: "Handel and his English Contemporaries, c. 1715 - 1760". p. 1

Words you do not know

There are various words in this paragraph you might not know, such as *Te Deum* and *Jubilate*. If you look such words up in a dic-tionary or encyclopedia, you might find out something interesting that could be relevant for your essay.

A useful tip about following 'trails'

Make sure you are not going up a blind alley when you follow a trail. Stop following a trail if it does not look as though you will get anywhere.

9 More about writing

When you have written a few essays and are writing essays that count towards your degree, you will need to make them extra-specially good. This chapter teaches you how to be self-critical so that you can really shine.

First, write your essay early. Then put it aside for a few days. Return to it as the deadline approaches. Read it through to see if it still makes as much sense to you as it did when you first wrote it. Ask yourself questions about the essay. Does it communicate what you thought it did when you first wrote it? Would someone else understand it easily? Most of all, ask:

Have I answered the question?

In Chapter 2, 'Looking at questions', we saw that questions did not look for a particular answer. We saw that the **coherence** of the argument was the most important part of the essay, not the point that was argued. 'Coherence' means that all the elements of the essay are pulling in the same direction. The three elements of an essay are:

■ opinion;

■ evidence;

■ brevity.

> *Remember!*
> An essay is your opinion about a little bit of a subject, in which you use evidence to support your opinion.

One frequent comment made about an undergraduate essay is that it does not answer the question. To answer the question, you need to have all three of these elements in balance, and it must also refer to the title.

As you read through your essay, you should be reading about your **opinion** and why it is valid based upon the **evidence** you have found. As you look out for these factors, ask yourself two more important questions:

- Does your **opinion** cover the same concerns as the question?

- Does your **evidence** apply to your opinion?

If the answer to either question is no, then you have not answered the question.

Examples

- You are writing on the essay title: 'Discuss the importance of the Tizer brand and its role in the development of the marketing mix'.

Your **opinion** is that the Tizer brand is very successful, and your **evidence**, based on research into various advertising campaigns, shows that the brand is one of the most successful soft drinks in the UK.

You have **not** answered the question. Your **evidence** is in order, but your **opinion** does not explore the role of the brand name in the 'marketing mix'.

The 'marketing mix' in the title includes other factors in the company strategy to sell the product. The question asks you to evaluate the Tizer brand, but if you ignore the brand's relationship to the rest of the 'marketing mix', you have only gone half way to fulfilling what has been asked. However good your **evidence**, if your **opinion** does not have any bearing on what the question is after, you have not answered the question.

- You are answering the question: 'To what extent can it be argued that Byron and Keats are second-generation Romantic poets?'

Your **opinion** is that Byron and Keats are second-generation Romantic poets, and your **evidence** states that Keats and Byron do not write poetry that fits with the model of first-generation Romantic poets.

Title
↓
Opinion (what you think)
↕
Evidence (what you have found out)

Example

Tizer and the marketing mix

?

Tizer is successful
↕
Advertising campaigns

Example

Byron and Keats as second-generation
↓
Yes they are!

?

They did not write first-generation poetry

You have **not** answered the question. Your **evidence** does not back up your **opinion**.

Whether Keats and Byron are or are not thought to be second-generation Romantic poets is up to you to decide, but evidence that they did not write like first-generation Romantic poets does not mean that they were second-generation Romantic poets. They may have been poets of a completely different kind altogether.

Too much information

Another thing that tends to go wrong in undergraduate essays is that they bring in too much information. When you have researched and found a number of ideas, it is tempting to put all of them into your essay. This can lead to the argument being squeezed out in favour of a list of the facts you have found.

A list is not an essay, since an essay is an **opinion** based upon **evidence** about **a little bit of the subject**. Remember that **brevity** is the third element of the definition of an essay when you are reading through.

You are not trying to say everything there is to say about your subject. Put in the evidence that is relevant to making your argument—and no more. Extra information will be irrelevant, and will just waste your word allowance. An essay that is padded out in this way is easy for a marker to spot.

In effect what you are trying to do in each of the six paragraphs of your essay is to say the same thing—six times. The thing you are saying is your opinion; what will differ is the evidence you give in each paragraph to back up your opinion.

You will not waste the research you have done by leaving it out of an essay. It might be useful in an exam. It might just be interesting to know.

Drafting and redrafting

An essay is never complete. It can always be made better. You have to make it as good as it can be in the time you have available.

At this stage you might still feel that there could be improvements. This is when you can feel very alone. Writing is one of the few things people do alone—even though it is for the purpose of communication. If you feel dissatisfied with your ideas, you could always try the following strategies.

Talk about the essay before you write it

When planning your essay, you might like to discuss it to make sure that your argument is going to work. When you have chosen which evidence you are going to use, and have finished your introduction, make an appointment to see your tutor. Do not take a first draft, just the introduction and the evidence. If you have talked about your strategy for arguing beforehand, you will feel more able to respond to the comments you get when you have written the essay.

Show your finished essay to someone

When you have written a first draft of your essay and read it through, you might find that you like what you have written. It is a good idea at this stage to give it to someone else to read. Do not choose a person on your course; find someone who knows nothing about what your topic, but whose judgement you can trust.

If they cannot understand it, it may be because you are trying to be too complex. Always try to be as clear and concise as you can, so that your essay is as easily comprehensible as it can be.

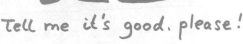

Tell me it's good, please!

It is always a good idea to get someone else to read through your essay before you submit it.

| # Some common errors to look out for

Lecturers and tutors throughout the country see errors like these regularly.

Long sentences

> Some people think it is a sign of intellectual achievement to write long, compound sentences, full of difficult and obscure words, and with spiralling sub-clauses, which, it is claimed, are the only vehicles for the maintenance of the required level of academic precision, while at the same time also allowing space for comprehension in a single stroke, like that of light striking 'upon the figured leaf', and hence such sentences bring together the divergent oppositional syntagmatic structures at micro and macro levels, so necessary for the undergraduate essay.

Long sentences (like the last one) can be wholly incomprehensible to readers.

What to do with long sentences

One problem with the long sentence above is that you need to read it three times (at least) to understand what it is trying to say. The sentence that follows it has twelve words. It is also much clearer than the first. So write short sentences.

How to write for your reader

As far as the long sentences above is concerned, you might redraft it thus:

> Some people think long words and sentences are the best for undergraduate essays. The argument is based on two ideas. First, long words and sentences are claimed to be models of academic precision. In other words, they function in the same way as a microscope. Details that are not at first visible become clear. This might be called the long sentence functioning on a 'micro' level. Second, long sentences are also said to give a total picture.

That is to say, long sentences act like a wide-angle camera lens, which might capture the view of a whole town in a single shot. This would be termed the long sentence functioning on a 'macro' level. By doing both at once, sentences constructed of long words are thought best.

What you will also have noticed is that the argument in this breakdown of the long sentence is not only easier to read; it is also clearer on the details, and gives a clearer 'total picture'. It also takes up more words, so will fill up your word count more quickly.

If you find you have long sentences in the draft of your essay, break them up into their component pieces.

Long words

Another problem with the long sentence in the example is that your reader might need to look up some of the words in a dictionary in order to understand them.

divergent oppositional syntagmatic structures at micro and macro levels

This is horrible.

A 'syntagmatic structure' is a sentence: say so.

'Divergent' sentences are sentences that say different things: say so.

'Micro and macro levels' are details and whole pictures: say so.

Do not hide what you are trying to say in long words or jargon.

Use readily readable words when you can.

Long words

If you use a long word, explain it carefully on the first use. Do not just give the dictionary definition. Say what you mean when you use it.

| # Another strategy for writing essays

In Chapter 4, we looked at a method of writing an essay by working out what you were going to argue, and writing an introduction which encapsulated it. It is sometimes the case that you do not know exactly what you want to argue until you have argued it. If this is the case you will need another strategy for writing your essay.

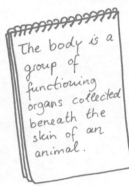

The body is a group of functioning organs collected beneath the skin of an animal.

Writing the body first

If you still feel at a loss about what you are going to argue after you have gathered your evidence, and cannot think of what your opinion might be, try writing a couple of paragraphs from the body of the essay.

In Chapter 4, we learned that each paragraph should:

- present some evidence;
- say where the evidence came from (**context**);
- then say why that evidence is part of the argument (**comment**).

Paragraph:
Evidence plus
Context plus
Comment

Introduction:
Opinion plus
Context

Paragraph:
Evidence plus
Context plus
Comment

This procedure was to make sure you remained relevant to your introduction throughout your essay.

It is also possible to **reverse the process**. If you write a paragraph which:

- presents some evidence;
- says where the evidence came from (**context**);
- then says why that evidence is part of an argument (**comment**),

then you can use what you have written to construct the introduction.

While you are writing the paragraph, ask yourself why you think the evidence is interesting, and what you are trying to argue. The answer to this question will then be the introduction.

Example

You have been gathering information for the topic:

■ Explain Harriet Martineau's role in the creation of sociology as a science.

You have found out from Michael Hill's essay on Martineau in *Women in Sociology* (1991) that she travelled to the Middle East, and made comparative surveys of people. What has caught your eye is the statement that 'before Marx, Engels or Weber, Martineau examined social class, religion, suicide, national character, domestic relations, women's status, criminology, and interrelations between institutions and individuals'. This looks interesting, but does not seem to have anything to do with science

You discover that she wrote up her findings from the Middle East in 1848, in a book called *Eastern Life Past and Present*, following the method she had laid out in an earlier book, her writings in *How to Observe Morals and Manners* (1838). This earlier book, you discover, offered a 'positivist' solution to certain problems of sociology.

Begin to write:

Michael Hill informs us that Martineau travelled to the Middle East in the early 1840s, studying the population in terms of

social class, religion, suicide, national character, domestic relations, women's status, criminology, and interrelations between institutions and individuals.

But in presenting her information (in *Eastern Life Past and Present*), this early woman sociologist did not merely present her facts in random order. On the contrary, she followed the precepts she herself had laid out in her earlier book, *How to Observe Morals and Manners.* This attention to method shows Martineau writing in a scientific way about subject matter which had hitherto not been thought of as scientific.

Such a paragraph would support the view that Harriet Martineau had indeed some role in creating sociology as a science. She had laid out an ordered method of study, and followed it herself in her later work. The degree to which her findings were accepted would also be necessary for the argument, but this paragraph suggests what the introduction might argue: that Harriet Martineau's role in the creation of sociology as a science lay in her methodological rigour.

The introduction may be a while in coming. You might have to write two or three, maybe four paragraphs, until it becomes clear, but when it does, write the introduction.

A warning about writing this way

If you choose to write this way (and it is a perfectly reasonable way to write an essay) you must go through all the paragraphs you have written **after** you have written the introduction to make sure all of them are part of the same argument. Do not present six 'essaylets' with an introduction to just one of them.

When you have chosen what your opinion is, you might have to rewrite other paragraphs so that the evidence is all used to back up the same opinion and to reach the same conclusion.

10 Dissertations and long essays

In many institutions, two modules in the third year of a full-time degree are given over to an extended piece of work, called a dissertation or long essay. This means you have a whole year to write it.

In part-time degrees, you will probably tackle it last and over a year also.

What is a dissertation?

A dissertation is a long essay written on a single topic, which you research by yourself. A member of staff will supervise progress, and be available to assist you.

Going about writing a long essay or dissertation is similar to writing an essay, but there are a number of differences.

■ You can choose your own title.

■ A dissertation is about five times longer than an ordinary essay.

■ Research should take you further afield than your institution's library.

Choosing a topic

Choosing your own topic sounds very exciting, but it can also be very daunting. You should start thinking about your topic before the long vacation of your second year of a full-time degree (the long vacation before you begin the dissertation if you are studying part-time). There are several criteria for your choice:

- Is the topic academic enough?

- Is the topic broad enough/too broad?

- Is the topic relevant to your degree course?

- Is there enough published material available on your topic?

- Will the topic keep you interested for a whole year?

My thoughts, such as they are, come crowding in so fast upon me, that my only difficulty is to choose or reject.
(Dryden)

Keeping interested

The last question might sound facetious, but is probably the most important. You will have to work on this subject for the summer vacation, and for at least one day a week for the two semesters of the final year of your degree.

When making your choice, the first thing you should do is ask yourself:

What made me choose the degree I am doing?

Whatever aspect of the subject made you make your choice of degree is probably the best place to start.

- You might have chosen to read Geography because you liked fell-walking.

- You might have chosen to read American Studies because you liked a film of an Edith Wharton novel.

- You might have chosen to read Business Studies because your family ran a shop.

When you have an idea, make an appointment to see your dissertation supervisor and discuss the other questions.

The **first part** of your dissertation will be a chapter explaining the analytical tools you are going to use and why they are relevant to your topic.

The **next three parts** of your dissertation will give evidence from different perspectives, following the analytical tools you have set up in the first chapter.

Is the topic academic enough?

Almost **any** topic can be academic.

It is not the **topic** itself but the **analysis** of the topic that makes it academic. However seemingly unacademic your idea may be, try it out with your supervisor.

If you think your topic is banal, try to have a back-up just in case.

Is the topic broad enough/too broad?

As with essays, dissertations need to say a lot about a little.

Like an essay, what you will need to do is to narrow down what you are going to say to get depth.

However, since you have more space, you will be able to give a number of sets of evidence, which will go to make up the argument of the whole dissertation.

Is the topic relevant to your degree course?

The point of a dissertation is to use one or two of the methods of study you have learned on your degree course.

What you must try to do is choose a topic that you can analyse using the methods you found most easy or interesting. This will make the topic relevant to your degree course.

Do not choose a topic you have studied on your degree course.

Is there enough published material available on your topic?

You will need to build up a fair-sized bibliography (about twenty items) for your dissertation. Begin using the methods described above and throughout this book; but it will look better if you go further afield than your institution's library to find materials.

You might even consider buying books for this project, since you may need a few by your side.

Searching further afield

To find out whether there is enough published material on your topic, you will need to consult several up-to-date bibliographical sources. Your institution's library will have electronic access to many of these relevant to your degree course. You need to search databases which give lists of books *and* articles.

For example:

■ British Humanities Index;

■ Bath Information and Data Service;

■ British Library Public Catalogue.

Ask at your library information desk for help in finding sources.

Try to gather these books and papers together prior to the long vacation before you write your dissertation. Then you will have time to read through them and begin to narrow down your idea when you return to semester time.

You will probably have to use inter-library loans, and maybe pay for papers to be photocopied for you. This will look very good in your bibliography, so no effort is wasted.

Remember!
You are not looking for specific books, but anything on your topic that looks as though it might be interesting.

Your title

When you get started on your dissertation, the first thing to do, as you are reading through the material you have gathered, is to try to think exactly what you want to argue in your dissertation.

As you are reading through the books on your topic, ask yourself:

■ What do I want to say about my topic?

Try to answer in a sentence of less than ten words.

This will be your title.

For example

You start off deciding to write about the representation of masculinity in twentieth-century American cinema.

You decide you are going to use a psychoanalytic analysis of the films.

You narrow down the films you are going to discuss to:

Citizen Kane
Tootsie
Dances with Wolves

See the films several times, read around in psychoanalytic film theory.

Ask yourself:
What do I want to say?

Answer:
I want to say that masculinity is depicted as a struggle between the external self and the inner man in American cinema of the twentieth century.

A good title style
has a short, snappy
beginning, then
a colon, then
an explanation.

So your title might be:
Inside Out: Masculinity as a struggle between the external self and the inner man in American cinema of the twentieth century.

The little bit at the beginning is an arresting opening. It will get your reader's interest. The sentence after the colon is the description of what will follow. Try to encapsulate what you want to say in this way.

Structure of the dissertation

When you have worked out the title, you must work out the structure of your dissertation.

Dissertations are usually 10,000 words. It might seem a lot, so break this up into manageable sections.

- Introduction   1,000 words

- Theoretical chapter   2,000 words

- Evidential chapter 1   2,000 words

- Evidential chapter 2   2,000 words

- Evidential chapter 3   2,000 words

- Conclusion   1,000 words

Now, all you have to do is write four 2,000-word essays, add an introduction and conclusion, and you are there.

BUT a dissertation is not simply four essays fastened together. It is a Single Argument.

Progression of the argument

You should begin researching and writing your dissertation with the theoretical chapter. This will set the ground rules for the evidential chapters.

Theoretical chapter

This chapter should be like the introduction to an essay. It is longer, since you have more to say. What you are trying to do is lay out your opinion:

- that is, explain what you have said in the title.

Also, you need to say why your opinion is valid in the light of other work that has been done. In this chapter you do not need evidence.

- This chapter will have a lot of theoretical references.

*Your glazing
is new and
your plumbing's
strange,
But otherwise
I perceive no
change; And
in less than a
month, if you do
as I bid, I'd learn
you to build
a pyramid!*

(Kipling)

Evidential chapters 1, 2, and 3

These chapters should be like the body of the essay. They give the evidence for the validity of your opinion.

They differ from the body of a single essay since they need to show the **progression** of the **argument**.

For example

For our 'Masculinity in American films' dissertation, you might show progression in terms of the dates of the three films:

■ *Citizen Kane* could only hint that masculinity could be questioned in the 1940s.

■ *Tootsie* could begin to question masculinity in the 1980s.

■ *Dances with Wolves* gets most clearly to the question of masculinity in the 1990s.

*Know prudent
cautious
self-control is
wisdom's root.*

(Burns (who was known for
his heavy drinking))

Another way to argue your dissertation might be to show progression in terms of the fierceness of the struggle between the inside and the outside:

■ *Citizen Kane* shows the outer man in control.

■ *Tootsie* shows the outer man beginning to lose control.

■ *Dances with Wolves* shows the outer man giving up his desire for control.

Each new chapter needs its own stance that marks a progression from the last, so that the whole dissertation:

■ takes on a shape;

■ has a direction;

■ has a coherent argument throughout.

Each chapter, whether it be the theoretical chapter or the evidential chapters, ought to follow the structure of an essay as laid out above.

Introduction and conclusion

These should be written last.

The **introduction** should lay out the whole argument, and briefly state where the argument is going in the individual chapters. This will amount to 200 words on the whole project and 200 words on each of the chapters.

The **conclusion** should point out the weak points in the argument, but give an idea, say, why this argument is better than the alternatives.

Page layout and presentation

Your institution will have stringent requirements about page layout and presentation of dissertations. Follow them to the letter.

11 | Exams

Examinations are one of the few times in your life that you can legitimately show off.

This is the sort of positive thing you should be saying to yourself when you go into an exam.

In order to show off, you need to be like an international athlete: in other words, you need to be well prepared long before the event.

To do well in exams you need to be like an athlete, well prepared.

Well before the exams

The most important things you need to know before going into an exam are:

■ what form the paper will take;

■ which of the work you have done on the module the exam will cover.

You will find out this information by studying past papers.

Where to find past papers

Ask at the information desk of your institution's library, where past papers are kept.

Take copies of the **two** most recent exams.

Take care not to look at the question on one of them.

Put it away to use as a test paper later.

What to look for on past papers

The information you need from the other exam paper is:

1. how long the paper is;

2. how many questions you have to answer;

3. what the conditions are for the examination.

The first two pieces of information will tell you **how long** you will have to write each answer. The third will tell you about the form of the exam.

The most usual length of exams are:

■ **ONE answer** in three-quarters of an hour, an hour, or an hour and a half;

■ **TWO answers** in two hours;

■ **THREE answers** in three hours.

When you know how many questions you have to do you can work out how much revising you will need to do.

The timing of examinations will vary from institution to institution. They may be placed at the end of the semester in an assessment period. They may be held at the end of the year in a special examination term, when there is no more teaching.

Examinations are formidable even to the best prepared, for the greatest fool may ask more than the wisest man can answer.

(Colton)

Enough if something from our hands have power to live, and act, and serve the future hour.

(Wordsworth)

Whenever they are, there never seems to be enough time to revise for them. However, it is worth bearing in mind that you can be too well prepared for an exam. If you go into the exam room able to answer all the questions on the paper, you will have a difficult decision which question to answer. You need to revise just enough to get through the exam comfortably. You want to be able to choose the questions you answer, but you do not have the time in an exam to choose between too many alternatives.

What you must do is work out what will be just enough revision.

What shall I revise?

Sometimes, essay questions for a module will cover work done in one part of the semester or term, and exams the work done in another.

It is also possible that both exams and essay questions will cover work done over the whole semester, term, or year.

Find out from your lecturer which work you have done will be covered by exam questions.

If you find that essays and exams happen to cover the same material:

In the exam, do not repeat material you wrote in an essay

When it comes to calculating your degree result, the external examiner will have access to all your work. If they see you have repeated material, your degree classification can be lowered.

Reading maketh a full man: … and writing an exact man.

(Bacon)

Calculating how much to revise

Calculate how many topics that you have to revise from:

■ the number of questions in the exam;

■ the number of topics you have covered;

■ the number of questions you have to answer in the exam.

Example

If there are:

- **twelve questions** in the exam;

- you have covered **twelve topics**;

- you have to answer **three questions**;

you will have to revise three topics to be certain that what you revised will come up. So revise **four** and you will have a choice. **Do not bother** to revise all twelve topics. You will not have time.

Another example

If there are:

- **five questions** in the exam;

- the module covers **six topics**;

- you have to answer **two questions**;

you will have to revise three topics to be certain that what you have revised will come up. So revise **four** topics to make sure you have a choice.

You may revise a topic on which there is no question.

Just before the exams

When you know how many topics you have to revise to be sure what you have revised will come up, set yourself a **work schedule**. Base the work schedule around the **conditions of the examination** (the third piece of information you got from the past paper).

Remember!
It is possible to do too much revision for an exam. Try to work out as well as you can how much revision you have to do, so you have a choice, BUT SO YOU CAN ALSO REVISE IN DEPTH.

Specific conditions for the examination

Check the past paper and find out whether:

- you are allowed to take books or other materials into the exam room
  - ○ open book exams;

- the questions for the exam will be made available to you before the exam
  - ○ open question exams.

Open book exams

If you are allowed to take books into an exam room, you will be expected to take information from them. In exams you do not have to give footnotes.

Problems with open book exams

You might think you will be allowed to write notes in your book. You cannot. If you are found with notes in your book you will be deemed to have cheated and all your exam marks will be nullified.

You might think you do not have to revise if you have the book in front of you. You do. You still have to know the text and where to look for quotes

Open question exams

If you are allowed access to the questions before the examination, you will be expected to have researched the exam (or part of the exam) in the same way as you research an essay. This means:

- There must be close references to sources.

- You will have to have thought up a good argument.

Your revision schedule

With these thoughts in mind, write out your work schedule. Exams are intended to be stressful. This is so that your work can be judged when you are pressed for time.

Exams are usually taken over one or two weeks. For example, your exam schedule for a typical degree programme of four modules might look like this:

Exam Schedule
Exam week 1:
Exam week 2: Exams for A,B,C
Exam week 3: Exam for D

A schedule such as this makes it look as though there is no time at all, so expand your programme into a day-to-day timetable:

Assessment Week 1	Assessment Week 2	Assessment Week 3
Mon	Mon: Exam A	Mon: Exam D
Tue	Tue	Tue
Wed	Wed: Exam B	Wed
Thu	Thu	Thu
Fri	Fri: Exam C	Fri
Sat	Sat	Sat
Sun	Sun	Sun

You will probably only just have finished an essay before the exam period begins. Take the weekend off before the first assessment week. Go and do your favourite things and relax. There is no point in trying to concentrate when you are tired.

Revision technique

Start work on your revision fresh and bright. And remember two things:

All clean and comfortable I sit down to revise.

(Keats (nearly))

■ This is revision.
  ○ DO NOT START READING NEW THINGS NOW.

■ You cannot concentrate for more than two hours at one stretch.
  ○ Separate your day into blocks of two hours with spaces for relaxation in between.

Revision: the three stages

What you are aiming to do for the topics you have chosen:

FIRST: Take **short notes** from the notes you took during the teaching weeks:

■ in lectures, seminars, reading for seminars.

This will get the ideas and arguments back into your head.

SECOND: Take shorter notes from your short notes.

■ Make cards with **headings** on that will remind you of the topic and its complexities.

Use these to go over the topics right up until you go into the exam room.

THIRD: Do an exam paper under exam conditions.

■ Use this to prove you are in tip-top condition.

Use the other exam paper you copied from the library, and sit the whole exam as though it was the real thing.

Exam nerves

Keep as relaxed as possible.

■ Take long periods of rest and quietness.

■ Eat well.

■ Do not drink alcohol.

During your revision time, work either in the library or at home. BUT DO NOT LET YOURSELF BE DISTURBED. Refuse if anyone asks you to go for a coffee. If you have children, lock yourself in your work room and arrange childcare for the two-hour blocks when you are working. Visits out and long walks for the children are a good idea, so their noise will not disturb you.

Do not let yourself be disturbed.

■ Refuse to go for a coffee.

■ Lock yourself in your work room.

■ Arrange childcare for your children if relevant.

The revision schedule itself

Break your day up into two-hour blocks.

Where you have the first two-hour block to revise for an exam:

■ Take **short notes** from your notes on the required number of topics.

Where you have two exams in a two-hour block:

■ Write out your **heading** cards.

On the day before each exam:

■ Sit a test exam.

Your exam work schedule should look something like this:

Of seeming arms to make a short essay, Then hasten to be drunk, the business of the day.

(Dryden)

Exam Week 1 a.m./p.m.
Mon: Revise A/ Revise B
Tue: Revise C/ Revise D
Wed: Revise A/ Revise B
Thu: Revise C/ Revise D
Fri: Revise AB/ Revise CD
Sat: REST
Sun: Test Exam A

Exam Week 2
Mon: Sit Exam A
Tue: Test Exam B
Wed: Sit Exam B
Thu: Test Exam C
Fri: Sit Exam C
Sat: REST
Sun: Test Exam D

Exam Week 3
Mon: Sit Exam D
Tue: REST!

Arrange the two-hour blocks at any time that suits you. Say, one block in the morning and one in the afternoon or early evening.

Do not work late into the night. You will forget things you try to learn late at night.

| # Exam room technique

When you are told you may begin:

■ Read the exam instructions very carefully.

■ Read through the whole paper quickly to get an idea of what each question entails before beginning to work on one of them.

■ Answer the easiest first, it will build up your confidence.

Writing exam answers you should follow the same rules as for writing an essay:

■ Think hard how you are going to answer the question, and make notes.

■ Write a long introduction stating your opinion and which material you will cover.

■ Then use evidence to show why your opinion is valid.

KEEP YOUR WATCH OR A CLOCK ON THE DESK IN FRONT OF YOU.

If you have **an hour** to write each answer:

■ Use **15 minutes** to devise how you are going to answer, making notes.

■ Write for **40 minutes**.

■ In the last **5 minutes** go through your answer and check it for spelling mistakes and ungrammatical sentences.

If you have **45 minutes** to write each answer:

■ Use **10 minutes** to devise how you are going to answer, making notes.

■ Write for **30 minutes**.

■ In the last **5 minutes** go through your answer and check it for spelling mistakes and ungrammatical sentences.

Be prepared

15 or 10 minutes' preparation may seem like a long time, and you might be tempted to start straight away, but preparation is vital and should not be rushed.

When there is more than one question

When you near the end of your allotted time for an answer, finish the answer you are doing as quickly as you can and go on to the next even if you have to rush the first.

You must complete all questions in the available time. Examiners can only mark what they see; they cannot mark good intentions.

> **Remember!**
> Each question can only get you a certain number of marks, and you will lose more by leaving a question unfinished than by getting another in better shape.

Rough notes

Hand in ALL rough notes you have written with the exam paper; they might help your examiner understand your answer.

Illness during exams

If you feel unwell during an exam put up your hand and tell the invigilator (the proctor), who will note the fact on your paper. When the exam is over **go to your doctor** and get a **medical certificate** to notify your institution of your symptoms and the date.

If you have to leave an exam due to severe illness, **go to your doctor immediately** and get a doctor's note.

Do not panic.

You might EITHER be allowed to sit the exam again, as though for the first time, OR a dip in your expected mark might be ignored when it comes to calculating your degree result.

> **Remember!**
> If you want illness during an exam to be taken into account, **you** must write a letter explaining your case, **and** have a doctor's note.

Exam room nerves

Before going into the exam, read through your note cards to refresh your memory of the salient facts. Breathe deeply and do some stretches. Avoid talking about the exam with other students.

If you have difficulty working in a crowded room, arrangements may be made for you to sit the exam in another room. Ask about this possibility **well in advance of the exam**.

Part B: Reference section
Contents

The purpose of the essay

The undergraduate essay is designed to show that you know about part of a subject area in some depth. It must also show that you can argue your case.

You should bear in mind three important elements of the essay:

Opinion:

This is your contribution. You do not have to say anything new, but must argue for a particular viewpoint.

Evidence:

This is the result of your research. The evidence you present should lead to the reasons why your opinion is to be believed.

Brevity:

An essay is not trying to say everything about a subject. You need to go into depth about just a little bit of the topic under discussion.

The essay question sheet

To help make your decision about which essay to choose:

Ask yourself, are the titles:

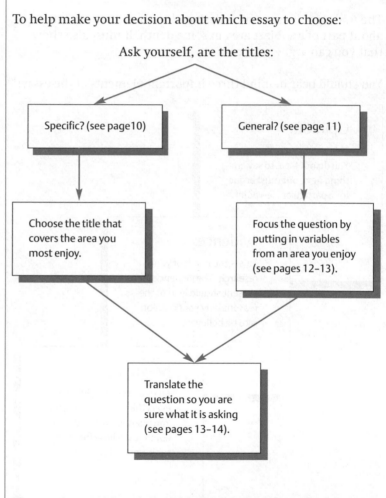

Specific? (see page10)

General? (see page 11)

Choose the title that covers the area you most enjoy.

Focus the question by putting in variables from an area you enjoy (see pages 12-13).

Translate the question so you are sure what it is asking (see pages 13-14).

Choose the question that you feel most confident about being able to answer and on which you are able to find evidence.

The process of research

Remember that research is not a search for a particular set of facts. Any fact you find interesting will probably be useful for your essay.

Find books

Use these methods to create your own reading list (see pages 23–4).

Take quotes

Quotes you might use in your essay will be those sentences you read that catch your eye.

When you take a quote, note down the details of the book you found it in:

■ author's name;

■ title of the book;

■ publication details (place: publisher, date);

■ page number.

Take notes

Notes will be pieces of information you might use for background information for your essay. They are not specific enough to be quoted. (See page 65.)

Form your opinion

Use the quotes and notes as evidence on which to base your opinion. What does the evidence suggest to you? (See pages 29–30.)

Develop your opinion

Write a short paragraph (say 100 words) stating what your opinion is. Make sure the evidence you have leads to your opinion. (See pages 30–1.)

Template for an essay

Introduction

(600 words)

Should contain:

■ information context of the topic;

■ your opinion;

■ critical framework.

Remember the phrase 'This essay will argue that …'

See pages 35–7.

You can write this section of the essay first

OR

you may prefer to write the body of the essay first and write the Introduction afterwards.

Body of the essay

(Six (or so) paragraphs of 200 words)

Each should contain:

■ evidence;

■ context—where does the evidence come from?

■ comment—how does the evidence fit your opinion?

See pages 37–9.

Conclusion

(200 words)

See pages 39–41.

Restatement of the argument, showing why it works and why it does not.

Drafting and redrafting

First draft

Get the words down on paper as fast as you can.

Begin from a paragraph if you are not sure what you want to argue.

Begin from the introduction if you are sure what you want to argue.

Second draft

See pages 43–5.

Make sure all paragraphs are made up of the relevant parts:

■ introductory statement;

■ quotation of evidence;

■ explanation of evidence;

■ statement of why the evidence fits your opinion.

See pages 45–6.

CHECK that your connecting words produce a logical argument:

Thus, Therefore, Nevertheless, Although, Furthermore, Still, But, However.

CHECK you have explained any new or unfamiliar words.

CHECK word count

Presentation checklist

It might be an idea to photocopy this page to use for the first few essays you write. Tick off the various elements when you have done them.

☐ double spacing

☐ wide margins

☐ font size (not less than 12 point)

☐ one side of the paper

☐ first page information

    ☐ title

    ☐ your name and identification number

    ☐ name of the module

☐ quotes separated from text/indented

☐ footnotes

☐ bibliography

☐ pages fastened together

Detailed resource sections

The next two sections give some detailed information about spelling and punctuation, and about footnotes and bibliographies. They are not exhaustive, but give enough information for an undergraduate essay. There is a list of resources at the end of the book.

Spelling and punctuation

Spelling

Try not to get spellings wrong, especially if you are copying from a book. If you are writing by hand, always check the spelling of any words you are not certain of, either in a dictionary or in the book in which you found the word.

If you have problems with spelling you can really help yourself if you word-process your essays. Almost all up-to-date word-processors have a spellchecker that you can switch on or off. It will automatically underline any misspelled words in red.

You will lose 5% from your total if you make more than a couple of mistakes in spelling, so a check is well worth doing.

A warning about computer spellcheckers

There is a hazard attached to spellcheckers. They do not underline words that may be spelled correctly, but which are wrong in context.

For example, the spellchecker will not underline any of these mistakes:

Were o were is the wicket which of the Vest?

It *should* read:

Where, oh where is the wicked witch of the West?

There is no easy solution to this problem, except for reading the essay over and over again.

Grammar

Grammar is the way words are put together to make a clear sentence that makes sense.

Grammar is also made easier in the days of the word-processor, since many now have a grammar-checker.

On most, the grammar-checker underlines things that are wrong in green. If you have trouble with grammar, it is a good idea to use a grammar-checker.

Problems with computer grammar-checkers

Once again you might still have problems even with both spelling and grammar-checkers switched on. They might not pick up certain things that are only wrong in context. Look out for the commonest errors as you read through your essay.

A few common errors

Proper names

When you use the spellchecker, almost all proper names:

- names of people

- names of places

- names of products

will be underlined in red as spelled wrong.

Do not think to yourself that the spellchecker just encountered a name and does not know it.

Make sure you have got it right.

Use the opportunity of the red line under the name you have typed to check **you** have spelled it correctly.

The apostrophe

There is a feeling in the air that the apostrophe is on its way
out. The idea is that it has become so misused that it will be
abandoned in the future. Until that day comes, however, you
must learn how to use it correctly.

What is the apostrophe for?

The **apostrophe** most often denotes **possession**: it means
that someone owns something.

It must **not** be used:

■ before the *s* in plural words

Vest's must be worn in the gym is wrong.

■ before the *s* in verbs

The river flow's to the sea is wrong.

If you want to show that someone owns something, use an
apostrophe and an *s*.

The boy owns the book.

Thus

It is the boy's book.

The boy owns the books.

Thus

They are the boy's books.

Plurals with apostrophes

What makes it a little harder is when there is an *s* at the end of
the word already. In the case of plurals it is not so difficult. Put
the apostrophe after the *s*.

The boys own the book

Thus

It is the boys' book.

The boys own the books.

Thus

They are the boys' books.

Names that end with an *s*

In the case of names that end with an *s* things are slightly more complicated. However, if you understand the logic of what you are doing, it is just the same as the other examples.

Charles Dickens wrote *Oliver Twist*.

Thus

It is Charles Dickens's book.

If you wrote: 'It is Charles Dicken's book', you would mean Charles Dicken wrote *Oliver Twist*. Which would not be correct.

Apostrophes in contractions

You can also use an apostrophe to mark contractions. This is when you shorten a word by leaving out letters.

For example:

Do not may be contracted into *Don't*.

There is only **one rule about contractions** in academic essays.

DO NOT USE CONTRACTIONS.

Always write words out in full.

Its and it's

In this case most of the rules seem to fly out of the window.
The correct thing is the reverse of what you would expect.

Its means the thing owned by it.

The dog sleeps in a red basket.

Thus

The dog sleeps in its red basket.

It's is the **contraction** for *it is*.

It is time to go home.

Thus

It's time to go home.

Since you should never use contractions in academic essays,
you should NEVER use *it's*.

A golden rule about *it's*
If you can write *it is*, and make sense, write *it is*. If not, then you
should use *its*. You will always be correct.

There, their, and they're

There is a place.

Point to it. Over **there**. Do you see?

Their is a possessive adjective.

The women have come on **their** bicycles.

They're is a contraction.

It means 'They are'.

DO NOT USE THEY'RE. Always write 'they are'.

To, too, and two

The best way to remember whether to use *to*, *too*, or *two* is to remember how to use the **three-lettered ones**.

Too is *too* much of a thing.

Examples:

It is 90 degrees. It is **too** hot.

It is zero degrees. It is **too** cold.

This coffee tastes weak. It is **too** watery.

Two is a number.

Examples:

Two is company. Three is a crowd.

The castle opens later. Shall we go at **two** o'clock?

In all other cases use 'to'.

Quotation marks

There are two sorts of quotation mark: 'single' and "double". They have different uses and must not be mixed up.

Single quotation marks

Use 'single' quotation marks when you want to draw your reader's attention to a word.

They are called 'scare' quotes. Use them if you are trying to make your reader aware that the word is special to your argument.

Examples:

For the purpose of this analysis of advertising strategies, the term 'impact' will be found to be vital.

This essay will argue that words such as 'interest', 'adamant' and 'gossip' have all changed significantly in meaning over the last two hundred years.

Double quotation marks

Use "double" quotation marks when you are putting a prose quote within the text of your essay.

Example:

We read in the *Daily Courant* of Friday, August 2, 1713, that "The Duke and Dutchess [*sic*] of Berry came last Tuesday to the Opera, ..." The duke and duchess were the centre of attention of that year's summer season in Paris.

Hyphens

Where there is more than one word in an adjective group that qualifies a noun, use a hyphen between the adjectives. These are called compound adjectives.

Example:

Eighteenth-century furniture is characterized by detailed woodcarving.

There is a hyphen here since 'furniture' is the noun, and 'eighteenth-century' is a compound adjective

BUT:

Carved wood is a common trait of the furniture of the eighteenth century.

There is no hyphen here, as 'century' is the noun.

Footnotes and bibliography

There are two common systems of putting references in your essay. They are called:

- Chicago;

- author–date.

It will depend on your institution, and perhaps on what you are writing about, which one you are required to use. Find out which one is required.

Do not mix up the two systems.

Footnotes and endnotes—Chicago style

The Chicago Manual of Style is now in its fourteenth edition. It is 921 pages long and will tell you **everything** you will ever need to know about laying out an essay or book.

This is a brief guide to the basics of noting the Chicago way. Your library will have a copy of the manual if you need more information.

Whenever you quote something:

- Put a superscripted number next to it.

- Write down the source
  - either at the bottom of the page (footnotes);
  - or the bottom of the essay (endnotes).

- Copy the source in the bibliography.

If you are word-processing your essay, you will find that the programme will organize footnotes or endnotes automatically.

Style for footnotes or endnotes

Quotes from books

These should give the following information, and in this order:

■ author or editor: full name, first name first;

■ *title: full title of book, including subtitle, in italics;*

■ translator (if any);

■ edition number (if it is not the first edition);

■ number of volumes (if it is a multi-volume work);

■ volume number from which the quote is taken;

■ facts of publication (city: publisher, date);

■ page number.

Examples:

Liam P. Unwin and Joseph Galloway, *Peace in Ireland* (Boston: Stronghope Press, 1990), 65.

John Caldwell, *The Oxford History of English Music*, 2 vols. Vol. 2 (Oxford: Oxford University Press, 1999), 1–3.

*Do not forget to put in the commas and full stops **exactly** as shown in the examples.*

Ibid.

If you have two quotes from the same book in subsequent footnotes, you can use the abbreviation 'Ibid.'

It is short for the Latin 'Ibidem', meaning 'in the same place'.

Other repeated citations

If you are repeatedly citing from the same text, you can make
up an abbreviation of your own, and put it in the footnote
or endnote.

Example:

> John Caldwell, *The Oxford History of English Music*, 2 vols. Vol. 2
> (Oxford: Oxford University Press, 1999). [Further citations to
> Caldwell will be shown thus: 'Caldwell,' followed by the page
> number.]

When you cite Caldwell again, your footnote would read,
for example:

> Caldwell, 64.

Quotes from articles in periodicals

These should give the following information, and in this order:

- author's name;

- 'Title of article' in quotation marks;

- *title of the periodical in italics*;

- issue information (volume number/issue);

- number (date);

- page numbers.

Examples:

> John J. Benjoseph, 'On the Anticipation of New Metaphors',
> *Cayahoga Review* 24 (1998): 6–10.

> John Feather, 'Cross-Channel Currents: Historical Bibliography and
> *l'histoire du livre*', *The Library* 6th Series, Volume II, No. 1 (March
> 1980): 1–15.

*Do not forget to put in the commas and full stops **exactly** as shown in
the example*s.

Quotes from films

These should give the following information, and in this order:

- *title in italics*;

- date;

- name of production company;

- place;

- name of director;

- (type of output) in brackets.

Example:

> *Citizen Kane*, 1941, RKO Radio, Hollywood, producer and director Orson Welles (motion picture).

Do not forget to put in the commas and full stops **exactly** *as shown in the example.*

Quotes from television programmes

These should give the following information, and in this order:

- 'title of the episode', in quotation marks;

- date of transmission;

- name of production company;

- place;

- (type of output) in brackets

Example:

> 'A Sheep called Dolly', 11 March 1997, *Heart of the Matter*, BBC Television, London (television programme).

Do not forget to put in the commas and full stops **exactly** *as shown in the examples.*

Quotes from the Internet

These should give enough information so that someone check-ing your source can find the exact page you quoted.

Example:

You have quoted from Deborah Barnes's essay 'Creating a Cloned Sheep called Dolly'.

Cite the whole Web address that will enable someone to retrieve the essay. Give the date on which you accessed the site, as information on websites does change.

http://science-education.nih.gov/nihHTML/ose/snapshots/
multimedia/ritn/dolly/ (accessed 7 July 2001)

REMEMBER: hyphens in web addresses look like decimal points. Spaces in web addresses are given by single underlines.

Example of Chicago-style noting

... and at this point, we notice that where Defoe writes, "and Chang'd the Generall [*sic*]",[1] George Harris Healey notes that

> The incompetent Duke of Schomberg, commanding British troops in Portugal, had just been relieved in favour of the Earl of Galway.[2]

From the informal way Defoe refers to Schomberg, as "the Generall", we can see the close relationship between Defoe and the Earl of Oxford ... .

[1] George Harris Healey, *The Letters of Daniel Defoe* (Oxford: Clarendon Press, 1955), 21.

[2] Ibid.

Bibliography

With the Chicago system of noting, you must supply a full bibliography **as well as** the list of notes.

If you have used endnotes at the end of your essay, put the bibliography **after** the endnotes.

The bibliography is nearly a repetition of the information in the notes, but there are subtle differences, mostly in the way you write names and in the punctuation.

Your note

Liam P. Unwin and Joseph Galloway, *Peace in Ireland* (Boston: Stronghope Press, 1990), 65.

This appears in the bibliography like this:

Unwin, Liam P., and Joseph Galloway. *Peace in Ireland*. Boston: Stronghope Press, 1990.

Your note

John Caldwell, *The Oxford History of English Music*, 2 vols. Vol. 2 (Oxford: Oxford University Press, 1999), 1–3.

This appears in the bibliography like this:

Caldwell, John. *The Oxford History of English Music*. 2 vols. Oxford: Oxford University Press, 1999.

Your note

John J. Benjoseph, 'On the Anticipation of New Metaphors', *Cayahoga Review* 24 (1998): 6–10.

This appears in the bibliography like this:

Benjoseph, John J. 'On the Anticipation of New Metaphors'. *Cayahoga Review* 24, 6–10.1998.

Your note

John Feather, 'Cross-Channel Currents: Historical Bibliography and *l'histoire du livre*', *The Library* 6th Series, Volume II, No. 1 (March 1980): 1–15.

This appears in the bibliography like this:

Feather, John. 'Cross-Channel Currents: Historical Bibliography and *l'histoire du livre*'. *The Library* 6th Series, Volume II, No.1, 1–15. March 1980.

Your note

Citizen Kane, 1941, RKO Radio, Hollywood, producer and director Orson Welles (motion picture).

This appears in the bibliography like this:

Citizen Kane. 1941. RKO Radio. Hollywood. Producer and director Orson Welles. (motion picture).

Your note

'A Sheep called Dolly', 11 March 1997, *Heart of the Matter*, BBC Television, London (television programme).

This appears in your bibliography like this:

Dolly. 'A Sheep called Dolly'. 11 March 1997. *Heart of the Matter*. BBC Television, London. (television programme).

*Do not forget to put in the commas and full stops **exactly** as shown in the examples.*

When you have finished preparing your bibliography entries, put **them in alphabetical order** by the first name that appears in the entry. List Internet sites separately.

Example bibliography

Bibliography

Benjoseph, John J. 'On the Anticipation of New Metaphors'.
Cayahoga Review 24, 6–10.1998.

Caldwell, John. *The Oxford History of English Music.* 2 vols.
Oxford: Oxford University Press, 1999.

Citizen Kane. 1941. RKO Radio, Hollywood. Producer and director
Orson Welles. (motion picture).

Dolly. 'A Sheep called Dolly'. 11 March 1997. *Heart of the Matter.*
BBC Television, London. (television programme).

Feather, John. 'Cross-Channel Currents: Historical Bibliography
and *l'histoire du livre*'. *The Library* 6th Series, Volume II, No.1,
1–15. March 1980.

Unwin, Liam P., and Joseph Galloway. *Peace in Ireland.* Boston:
Stronghope Press, 1990.

Internet websites

http://science-education.nih.gov/nihHTML/ose/snapshots/
multimedia/ritn/dolly/

Do not forget to
put in the commas
and full stops
exactly as shown in
the examples.

Author–date citations

The author–date method of citation uses abbreviations within
the text rather than footnotes. The abbreviations may then be
checked against a list of Works Cited.

When you reach the point in the text where the footnote
number would come, put in the abbreviation that will allow
your reader to find out exactly which text you are citing.

Abbreviations you put in the text include:

■ author;

■ date of publication;

■ page number (if any).

Examples:

(Benjoseph, 1998, 125)

(Caldwell, 1999, 1–3)

(*Citizen Kane*, 1941)

(Dolly, 1997)

(Feather, 1980, 14)

(Unwin, 1990)

Example of author–date style noting

... and at this point, we notice that where Defoe writes, "and
Chang'd the Generall [*sic*]", George Harris Healey notes that
(Healey, 1933, 21)

The incompetent Duke of Schomberg, commanding British
troops in Portugal, had just been relieved in favour of the
Earl of Galway.

From the informal way Defoe refers to Schomberg, as "the
Generall", we can see the close relationship between Defoe and
the Earl of Oxford ... .

Citation list

NOTE The list of
works cited is set
out differently from
the bibliography.

At the end of your essay, you put the list of works cited in
alphabetical order.

Works Cited

Benjoseph, John J. 1998. 'On the Anticipation of New Metaphors'. *Cayahoga Review* 24: 6–10.

Caldwell, John. 1999. *The History of English Music*. 2 vols. Oxford: Oxford University Press.

Citizen Kane. 1941. RKO Radio, Hollywood. Producer and director Orson Welles. (motion picture).

Dolly. 'A Sheep called Dolly'. 11 March 1997. *Heart of the Matter*. BBC Television, London. (television programme).

Feather, John. 1980. 'Cross-Channel Currents: Historical Bibliography and *l'histoire du livre*'. *The Library* 6th Series, Volume II, No.1, 1–15. March.

Unwin, Liam P., and Joseph Galloway 1990. *Peace in Ireland*. Boston: Stronghope Press.

Footnotes and bibliography

Do not forget to put in the commas and full stops **exactly** as shown in the examples.

121

List of resources

Some books you might find useful in helping you to write essays:

Fitzgerald, Sallyanne. *Essay Writing Simplified*. London: HarperCollins, 1993.

Dean, Kitty Chen. *Essentials of the Essay*. New York: Allyn and Bacon, 1998.

Redman, Peter. *Good Essay Writing: A Social Sciences Guide*. London: Sage, 2001.

Swetenham, Derek. *Writing your Dissertation*. London: How to Books, 2000.

Evans, Harold. *Essential English*. London: Pimlico, 2000.

Other books in the One Step Ahead series, in particular *Spelling*, *Words*, *Punctuation*, and *Editing and Revising Text* might be useful.

Some bibliographical websites you might find useful in your research:

The Annual Bibliography of English Language and Literature: www.lib.cam.ac.uk/MHRA/ABELL

The British Library
www.bl.uk

The Library of Congress
www.loc.gov

The Bodleian Library, Oxford
www.bodley.ox.ac.uk

Trinity College, Dublin
www.tcd.ie/Library

Cambridge University Library
www.lib.cam.ac.uk

Bath Information and Data Service
www.BIDS.ac.uk
(You will need your institution's password to use this service.)

British Humanities Index
www.BHInet.co.uk
(You will need your institution's password to use this service.)

Some useful websites that might help you write your essay:

www2.actden.com/writ_den/tips/essay/

www.powa.org

www.askoxford.com

Permissions

Sample bibliography on page 63 is taken from D. Craine and
J. Mackrell, *The Oxford Dictionary of Dance* (OUP, 2000).

Extracts on pages 27 and 66–7 are taken from John Caldwell,
The Oxford History of English Music, Vol. 2, chapter 1: 'Handel and
his English Contemporaries, *c*. 1715–1760' (OUP, 1999).

Index